The
Collected
Ghazals
of
Hafiz

The Collected Ghazals of Hafiz

With the Original Farsi Text,
English Translation, Transliteration and Notes

VOLUME FOUR

JAMILUDDIN MORRIS ZAHURI
WITH MARYAM MOGHADAM

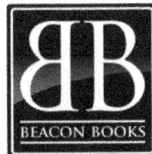

BB
BEACON BOOKS

Published by Beacon Books and Media Ltd
Innospace
The Shed
Chester Street
Manchester
M1 5GD
UK

www.beaconbooks.net

ISBN Volume 1   978-0-9954960-1-9
ISBN Volume 2   978-0-9954960-2-6
ISBN Volume 3   978-0-9954960-3-3
ISBN Volume 4   978-0-9954960-4-0
ISBN Full Set   978-0-9954960-0-2

A C.I.P. record for this book is available from the British Library

All artwork Jamiluddin Morris Zahuri
Cover design by Bipin Mistry

The present volume is the fourth of four volumes that (together with the appendix) contain the 573 poems of the entire collection of ghazals presented by Wilberforce-Clarke; of these 486 are in the main body of the four volumes and are accompanied by the original Farsi and a transliteration in 'roman' script. Some original verses by this writer are included in the introduction under the pen name *Zahuri*.

About this book

The Khwaja Hafiz Shirazi Foundation was originated by Dr Zahurul Hasan Sharib of Ajmer (d.1996) with the publication of '*Hafiz and His Rubaiyat*' *(Sharib Press, Southampton, 1993)*, being translations of the quatrains in that style by Hafiz Saheb. This work is being carried forward by the present author with the intention of presenting to a wider English language audience the much more extensive ghazals. This volume is therefore the second publication, linked to the foundation, to be completed. The full ghazaliyat is to be found in three subsequent volumes.

This book is primarily a rendition in rhyming couplets of the collected ghazals from the Divan of Khwaja Hafiz Shirazi, from English sources, by Jamiluddin Morris Zahuri. It is edited with reference to the original Farsi by Maryam Moghhadam of Shiraz.

Biographical

Dr Zahurul Hassan Sharib (1914-96); born in Moradabad, India, but passed much of his later life in Ajmer, India, where his study overlooked the shrine of the great Sufi Saint Khwaja Muinuddin Hasan Chishti. He published well over 100 books in English and Urdu mostly on Sufi themes but also on rural reconstruction. He was fluent in several languages including Farsi. He led the Gudri Shahi Order of Sufis from 1973 till his demise in 1996.

Jamiluddin Morris Zahuri; born in Hastings, Sussex, England, in 1946. He was trained in the Sufi tradition of the Chishti Order for over twenty years, from 1976, by Dr Sharib. He later received the benefit of the company of Hazrat Nuri Baba of Konya and still regularly visits the shrines of Khwaja Muinuddin Hasan Chishti in Ajmer and Mevlana Jalaluddin Rumi in Konya.

Originally trained in fine art, Jamil has lived in Southampton, England for the past 30 years with his Indian wife Farhana. He is the founder of Sharib Press, which has produced a dozen books on Islamic Mysticism and Qur'an Commentary. He has provided the design and art work for the present volume.

Now retired from practice as a therapist he writes poetry with a mystical theme and guides a number of followers on the Sufi path. Since 1998 he has run the Zahuri Sufi Website for which he has written many articles and poems. (zahuri.org)

Contents

Tomb of Hafiz in Shiraz, Iran

Ghazaliyat

غزلیات

O you who have the stature to wear the cloak of sovereignty,
The crown gets lustre from the precious jewel[1] of your majesty.

Every moment the rising of the sun of victory takes place,
From the royal diadem that sits above your moon like face.

The sun in the sky may be the world's lamp and its eye,
But dust under your feet is the illumination of that eye.

The place where the auspicious bird makes manifest its glory,
Is wherever the Huma[2] shade falls from your sphere-like canopy.

Despite a thousand ways of understanding sacred law and philosophy,
Your wise heart never failed to distinguish a single point of subtlety.

The water of life drips from the beak of your eloquence in speaking,
That sweetly spoken parrot, I mean your reed pen, is sugar breaking.

What Alexander[3] desired but was denied by destiny,
Was a sip from your cup of life-bestowing purity.

No one need express a desire in the ambit of your presence,
No one's secret is hidden from the light of your intelligence.

Being only a slave in your presence, is the boast made by Hafiz,
Hoping that life-bestowing, world-forgiving clemency there is.

(W-C 467) See appendix.
(W-C 468) The radif here is "Of yours".
> [1] *"...jewel..." This word can also mean 'stock' and according to Avery could carry an allusion to the royal stock. We could, however, take the jewel to imply the divine spark if we understand majesty to refer to God. As with many of Hafiz's verses praising Kings there is the possibility of understanding it a disguise for praise of God.*
> [2] *"...Huma..." A legendary bird whose shadow brings good fortune to anyone it falls on.*
> [3] *"...Alexander..." See under 'Sikander' in the glossary in volume one.*

Ey ghabaaye paad shaahi raast bar baalaaye to
Taaje shaahi raa foroogh az govhare vaalaaye to

Aaftaabe fath raa har dam tolooee midahad
Az kolaahe khos roye rokhsaare mah simaaye to

Gar che khorshide falak chashmo cheraaghe aalam ast
Rovshanaaee bakhshe chashme oust khaake paaye to

Jelve gaahe taayere eghbaal gardad har kojaa
Saaye andaazad homaaye chatre gardoon saaye to

Dar rosoome shar o hekmat baa hezaaraan ekhtelaaf
Noktei hargez nashod fovt az dele daanaaye to

Aabe heyvaanash ze menghaare balaaghat michekad
Tootiye khosh lahje yani kelke shekkar khaaye to

Aanche eskandar talab kardo nadaadash roozegaar
Jore ee bood az zolaale jaame jaan afzaaye to

Arze haajat dar harime hazratat mohtaaj nist
Raaze kas makhfi namaanad baa forooghe raaye to

Hafez andar hazratat laafe gholaami mizanad
Bar omide afve jaan bakhshe jahaan bakhshaaye to

ای قبای پادشاهی راست بر بالای تو
تاج شاهی را فروغ از گوهر والای تو

آفتاب فتح را هر دم طلوعی می دهد
از کلاه خسروی رخسار مه سیمای تو

گر چه خورشید فلک چشم و چراغ عالم است
روشنائی بخش چشم اوست خاک پای تو

جلوه گاه طایر اقبال گردد هر کجا
سایه اندازد همای چتر گردون سای تو

در رسوم شرع و حکمت با هزاران اختلاف
نکته ای هرگز نشد فوت از دل دانای تو

آب حیوانش ز منقار بلاغت میچکد
طوطی خوش لهجه یعنی کلک شگرخای تو

آنچه اسکندر طلب کرد و ندادش روزگار
جرعه ای بود از زلال جام جان افزای تو

عرض حاجت در حریم حضرتت محتاج نیست
راز کس مخفی نماند با فروغ رای تو

حافظ اندر حضرتت لاف غلامی می زند
بر امید عفو جان بخش جهان بخشای تو

For the Chinese musk pod the dust of your path is blood money[1],
The sun grows in the shelter of the shade of one side of your topi.

Walk out proudly, the narcissus goes too far with flirty glances!
May my soul be sacrificed to your black eye and its glances.

Drink this blood of mine; for no angel seeing your beauty,
Will, in the record of sins, have the heart to make an entry.

To the people of the world you bring sleep and rest,
So the corner of my eye and heart is where I get rest.

I am in secret conference with every star, each night,
Sorrowfully longing for your moon-like face's light.

Our company has departed, each gone their separate way,
Only we, in the shelter of your fortune-giving threshold, stay.

Hafiz, don't despair of divine attention, in the end, inevitably,
Ignited by the smoke of your sigh the harvest of sorrow will be.

(W-C 469) The radif here is "Of yours".
[1] *"...blood money..." See under 'blood price' in the glossary in volume one.*

Ey khoon bahaaye naafeye chin khaake raahe to
Khorshid saaye parvare tarfe kolaahe to

ای خونهای نافه چین خاک راه تو
خورشید سایه پرور طرف کلاه تو

Narges kereshme mibarad az had boroon kharaam
Ey jaan fadaaye shiveye chashme siyaahe to

نرگس کرشمه می برد از حد برون خرام
ای جان فدای شیوه چشم سیاه تو

Khoonam bekhor ke hich malak baa chonaan jamaal
Az del nayaa yadash ke nevisad gonaahe to

خونم بخور که هیچ ملک با چنان جمال
از دل نیایدش که نویسد گناه تو

Aaraamo khaabe khalghe jahaan raa sabab toee
Zaan shod kenaare didevo del tekye gaahe to

آرام و خواب خلق جهان را سبب توئی
زان شد کنار دیده و دل تکیه گاه تو

Baa har setaarei saro kaarist har shabam
Az hasrate forooghe rokhe hamcho maahe to

با هر ستاره ای سر و کاریست هر شبم
از حسرت فروغ رخ همچو ماه تو

Yaaraane hamneshin hame az ham jodaa shodand
Maaeemo aastaaneye dovlat panaahe to

یاران همنشین همه از هم جدا شدند
مائیم و آستانه دولت پناه تو

Hafez tama mabor ze enaayat ke aaghebat
Aatash zanad be kharmane gham doode aahe to

حافظ طمع مبر ز عنایت که عاقبت
آتش زند به خرمن غم دود آه تو

O you, merely the mirror holder for your beauty, the sun is,
For your mole, the incense holder that's passed round, musk is.

I cleaned the yard of the eye's palace, but what's the point?
Not suitable for the army of your imagination is this joint.

You have ascended to the zenith of tenderness, O sun of beauty,
O Lord! Until the day of Resurrection no setting let there be.

Never before has there been an image made with so much beauty,
By the seal scribe who delineated your eyebrow, black and musky.

In the curl of the beloved's hair, my heart, how are you getting on?
For the dawn breeze has told me that you are in a state of confusion.

The rose's scent is pervasive, reconciliation let there be,
You face is our good fortune and our spring's augury.

So that the heavens may wear our ring of slavery ,
Where is your crescent eyebrow's hint of coquetry.

So that, with felicitations, to a good fortune I may be returning,
Where is the good news that the festival of our union is coming.

The black spot which has become the locus of light,
Is a reflection of your mole in the garden of our sight.

In the presence of the ancient which tyranny to mention,
My own state of need or the offence that you have taken?

Hafiz, so many disobedient heads this noose is catching,
About what you cannot realise, don't bother fantasising.

(W-C 470) The radif here is "Of yours".
    [1] "...rings of slavery..." The status of slavery was marked by a ring worn in the ear.
    [2] "...the black spot..." The black spot here is probably the eye's pupil. See in the glossary in volume one for 'mole'.

Ey aaftaab aayene daare jamaale to
Moshke siyaah mejmare gardaane khaale to

ای آفتاب آینه دار جمال تو
مشک سیاه مجمره گردان خال تو

Sahne saraaye dide beshostam vali che sood
Kin gooshe nist dar khore kheyle khiyaale to

صحن سرای دیده بشستم ولی چه سود
کاین گوشه نیست در خور خیل خیال تو

Dar ovje naazo nemati ey aaftaabe hosn
Yaa rab mabaad taa be ghiyaamat zavaale to

در اوج ناز و نعمتی ای آفتاب حسن
یا رب مباد تا به قیامت زوال تو

Mat bo tar ze naghshe to soorat nabast baaz
Toghraa nevise abrooye moshkin mesaale to

مطبوع تر ز نقش تو صورت نبست باز
طغرانویس ابروی مشکین مثال تو

Dar chine zolfash ey dele ghamgin chegoonei
Kaashofte goft baade sabaa sharhe haale to

در چین زلفش ای دل غمگین چگونه ای
کاشفته گفت باد صبا شرح حال تو

Bar khaast booye gol ze dare aashti dar aay
Ey nov bahaare maa rokhe farkhonde faale to

برخاست بوی گل ز در آشتی درآی
ای نوبهار ما رخ فرخنده فال تو

Taa aasemaan ze halghe be gooshaane maa shavad
Koo eshvei ze abrooye hamchon helaale to

تا آسمان ز حلقه بگوشان ما شود
کو عشوه ای ز ابروی همچون هلال تو

Taa pishe bakht baaz ravam tahniyat konaan
Koo mojdei ze maghdame eide vesaale to

تا پیش بخت باز روم تهنیت کنان
کو مژده ای ز مقدم عید وصال تو

In noghteye siyaah ke aamad madaare noor
Aksist dar hadigheye binesh ze khaale to

این نقطه سیاه که آمد مدار نور
عکسیست در حدیقه بینش ز خال تو

Dar sadre khaaje arze kodaamin jafaa konam
Sharhe niyaazmandiye khod yaa malaale to

در صدر خواجه عرض کدامین جفا کنم
شرح نیازمندی خود یا ملال تو

Hafez darin kamand sare sar keshaan basist
Sovdaaye kaj mapaz ke nabaashad majaale to

حافظ درین کمند سر سرکشان بسیست
سودای کج مپز که نباشد مجال تو

On the life of the tavern's Elder[1], and right to gratitude he has,
Except to be of service to him no other thought my mind has.

Though paradise is no place for sinners to be residing,
Bring wine, for I am certain of his attentive regarding[2].

May the lightning lamp from that thunder cloud be lit,
That with love's fire struck our life's harvest and burnt it.

Bring wine, for last night, from the unseen, a messenger came,
With the news that the divine bounty for everyone is the same.

If, on the threshold of the tavern, you find a head lying there,
Don't kick it, for hid from you is its purpose in being there.

Don't look at a drunkard like me contemptuously,
Without Divine Will there is neither sin nor piety.

Always in hock for wine, is the Sufi robe of Hafiz,
It seems made from the tavern's dust his nature is,

Our heart doesn't really care much for repentance or piety,
But I try in the name of the Elder and his fortune and glory.

(W-C 471) The radif here is "of his (or of His)".
[1] *"...the Elder..." The Pir, or spiritual guide. Generally speaking Pir is often used to denote one of higher spiritual status but usage varies.*

Be jaane pire kharaabaato hagh ghe nemate ou
Ke nist dar sare maa joz havaaye khedmate ou

به جان پیر خرابات و حقّ نعمت او
که نیست در سر ما جز هوای خدمت او

Behesht agar che na jaaye gonaah kaaraanast
Biyaar baade ke mos tazharam be hemmate ou

بهشت اگرچه نه جای گناهکاران است
بیار باده که مستظهرم به همّت او

Cheraaghe saa-egheye aan sahaab rovshan baad
Ke zad be kharmane maa aatashe mahabbate ou

چراغ صاعقه آن سحاب روشن باد
که زد به خرمن ما آتش محبّت او

Biyaar baade ke doosham sorooshe aalame gheyb
Navid daad ke aam ast feyze rahmate ou

بیار باده که دوشم سروش عالم غیب
نوید داد که عام است فیض رحمت او

Bar aastaaneye meykhaane gar sari bini
Mazan be paay ke ma-loom nist niyyate ou

بر آستانه میخانه گر سری بینی
مزن به پای که معلوم نیست نیّت او

Makon be chashme heghaarat negaah dar mane mast
Ke nist ma-siyato zohd bi mashiyyate ou

مکن به چشم حقارت نگاه در من مست
که نیست معصیت و زهد بی مشیّت او

Modaam khergheye Hafez be baade dar gerovast
Magar ze khaake kharaabaat bood tinate ou

مدام خرقه حافظ به باده در گرو است
مگر ز خاک خرابات بود طینت او

Nemikonad dele maa meyle zohdo tovbe vali
Be naame khaaje bekooshimo farre dovlate ou

نمی کند دل ما میل زهد و توبه ولی
به نام خواجه بکوشیم و فرّ دولت او

Your musk diffusing curl fills the violet full of envy,
Your heart expanding laughter opens the rosebud fully.

Don't burn your bulbul, my rose whose breath is kindly,
For all night and every night it prays for you sincerely.

I, who found even the angel's breath to be annoying,
All the arguing of the world, for your sake, I am bearing.

Love for your face is in my nature, your door's dust, my heaven;
My destiny is your love; if you are pleased my ease I find then.

The sleeve of the patched dress of love's beggar hides a treasure,
Sovereignty is quickly gained by one who becomes your beggar.

The throne of my eye is the high seat for your majesty,
It is good to pray there; O king may it never be empty.

The drunken craziness of your love-wine goes out of my mind,
When this desire-filled head of mine in your door's dust I find,

Your face is a garden of delight, especially in the spring of beauty,
Hafiz, your song bird has become one that sings its songs sweetly.

Look what fortune love shows, for regarding power and glory,
A poor beggar of yours tips askew the crown of sovereignty.

Though not going together, the wine cup and robe of austerity,
In order to satisfy you, I draw into a picture all this imagery.

(W-C 472) The radif here is "Of yours".

Taabe banafshe midahad torreye moshk saaye to
Pardeye ghonche midarad khandeye del goshaaye to

تاب بنفشه می دهد طرّه مشکسای تو
پرده غنچه می درد خنده دلگشای تو

Ey gole khosh nasime man bolbole khish raa masooz
Kaz sare sedgh mikonad shab hame shab doaaye to

ای گل خوش نسیم من بلبل خویش را مسوز
کز سر صدق می کند شب همه شب دعای تو

Man ke malool gashtami az nafase fereshtegaan
Ghaalo maghaale aalami mekesham az baraaye to

من که ملول گشتمی از نفس فرشتگان
قال و مقال عالمی می کشم از برای تو

Mehre rokhat sereshte man khaake darat beheshte man
Eshghe to sarnebeshte man raahate man rezaaye to

مهر رخت سرشت من خاک درت بهشت من
عشق تو سرنبشت من راحت من رضای تو

Dalghe gedaaye eshgh raa ganj bovad dar aastin
Zood be saltanat rasad hark e bovad gedaaye to

دلق گدای عشق را گنج بود در آستین
زود به سلطنت رسد هر که بود گدای تو

Shaah neshine chashme man tekye gahe khiyaale tost
Jaaye doaast shaahe man bi to mabaad jaaye to

شاه نشین چشم من تکیه گه خیال تست
جای دعاست شاه من بی تو مباد جای تو

Shoore sharaabe eshghe to aan nafasam ravad ze sar
Kin sare por havas shavad khaake dare saraaye to

شور شراب عشق تو آن نفسم رود ز سر
کاین سر پرهوس شود خاک در سرای تو

Khosh chamanist aarezat khaase ke dar bahaare hosn
Hafeze khosh kalaam shod morghe sokhan saraaye to

خوش چمنیست عارضت خاصه که در بهار حسن
حافظ خوش کلام شد مرغ سخن سرای تو

Dovlate eshgh bin ke chon az sare faghro eftekhaar
Goosheye taaje saltanat mishekanad gedaaye to

دولت عشق بین که چون از سر فقر و افتخار
گوشه تاج سلطنت می شکند گدای تو

Khergheye zohdo jaame mey gar che na dar khore hamand
In hame naghsh mizanam az jahate rezaaye to

خرقه زهد و جام می گرچه نه در خور هم اند
این همه نقش می زنم از جهت رضای تو

The moon was eclipsed by the down on the beloved's face,
It's a joyful ring, but no path out of it, is it possible to trace.

The friend's eyebrow, an arch over the prayer alcove[1] of fortune, is,
Rub your face there and ask from that one whatever your need is.

O drinker in the gathering of Jam[1]; keep your heart pure,
For the cup is a world revealing mirror. Oh dear, for sure!

From the path of love to the tavern the Sufi took me,
The smoke there has made my book black, just see.

To the demon of sorrow say – "Do whatever!"
From him with the wine vendors I took shelter.

Hold the wine cup in the sunbeam as a lamp, Saki,
Say, "Lit up from this lamp let the morning be!"

Sprinkle water on the record of what we do each day,
Maybe the recorded sins there can be washed away.

Hafiz, whoever brought harmony to the lover's meeting,
May that one never, ever, be absent from this gathering.

The city's beggar indulges in this fine fantasy,
About coming one day into the king's memory.

(W-C 473)
  [1] "...Jam..." Jamshid – see glossary in volume one.

Khatte ezaare yaar ke begreft maah azoo
Khosh halghe ist leek be dar nist raah azoo
خطّ عذار یار که بگرفت ماه ازو
خوش حلقه ایست لیک به در نیست راه ازو

Abrooye doost goosheye mehraabe dovlat ast
Aanjaa bemaal chehrevo haajat bekhaah azoo
ابروی دوست گوشه محراب دولت است
آنجا بمال چهره و حاجت بخواه ازو

Ey jor-e nooshe majlese jam seene paak daar
Kaaeene ist jaame jahaan bin ke aah azoo
ای جرعه نوش مجلس جم سینه پاک دار
کاینه ایست جام جهان بین که آه ازو

Soofi maraa be meykade bord az tarighe eshgh
In doode bin ke naameye man shod siyaah azoo
صوفی مرا به میکده برد از طریق عشق
این دوده بین که نامه من شد سیاه ازو

Sheytaane gham har aanche tavaanad begoo bekon
Man bor deam be baade forooshaan panaah azoo
شیطان غم هرآنچه تواند بگو بک
من برده ام به باده فروشان پناه ازو

Saaghi cheraaghe mey be rahe aaftaab daar
Goo bar forooz mash aleye sobh gaah azoo
ساقی چراغ می به ره آفتاب دار
گو برفروز مشعله صبحگاه ازو

Aabi be rooz naameye a-maale maa feshaan
Betvaan magar setord horoofe gonaah azoo
آبی به روزنامه اعمال ما فشان
بتوان مگر سترد حروف گناه ازو

Hafez ke saaze majlese osh shaagh raast kard
Khaali mabaad arseye in bazm gaah azoo
حافظ که ساز مجلس عشّاق راست کرد
خالی مباد عرصه این بزمگاه ازو

Aayaa dar in khiyaal ke daarad gedaaye shahr
Roozi bovad ke yaad konad paad shaah azoo
آیا درین خیال که دارد گدای شهر
روزی بود که یاد کند پادشاه ازو

The rosebud of delight blooms, but the rose-cheeked Saki is where?
The spring breeze is blowing but the fine taste of wine is where?

Every new rose reminds of a rose cheeked one who is fair,
But the listening ear is where? The seeing eye is where?

In the banquet hall of pleasure no scent of desire can one find there,
O sweet breath of dawn, the musk-pod of the beloved's hair is where?

The rose going on about the beauty it possesses, I simply cannot bear,
My hand on my heart's blood, for God's sake say, my beloved is where?

Arise! The dawn candle boasted of how like your face it does appear,
The foe's tongue has grown too long, the bright dagger is where?

"You want a kiss from my ruby lip?" asked the beloved one so fair.
I died to satisfy this desire, but my will and my power is where?

Though to guard the treasury of words of wisdom, Hafiz is there,
In these bad times the one who speaks flowingly of grief is where?

(W-C 474) The radif here is "Where?" We have made use of this.

Golbone eysh midamad saaghiye gol ezaar koo
Baade bahaar mivazad baadeye khosh gavaar koo

گلبن عیش می دمد ساقی گلعذار کو
باد بهار می وزد باده خوشگوار کو

Har gole nov ze gol rokhi yaad hami konad vali
Gooshe sokhan shenov kojaa dideye etebaar koo

هر گل نو ز گلرخی یاد همی کند ولی
گوش سخن شنو کجا دیده اعتبار کو

Majlese bazme eysh raa ghaaliyeye moraad nist
Ey dame sobhe khosh nafas naafeye zolfe yaar koo

مجلس بزم عیش را غالیه مراد نیست
ای دم صبح خوش نفس نافه زلف یار کو

Hosn forooshiye golam nist tahammol ey sabaa
Dast zadam be khoone del bahre khodaa negaar koo

حسن فروشی گلم نیست تحمّل ای صبا
دست زدم به خون دل بهر خدا نگار کو

Khiz ke sham-e sobh dam laaf ze aareze to zad
Khasm zabaan deraaz shod khanjare aab daar koo

خیز که شمع صبحدم لاف ز عارض تو زد
خصم زبان دراز شد خنجر آبدار کو

Goft magar ze la-le man boose nadaari aarezoo
Mordam azin havas vali ghodrato ekhtiyaar koo

گفت مگر ز لعل من بوسه نداری آرزو
مردم ازین هوس ولی قدرت و اختیار کو

Hafez agar che dar sokhan khaazane ganje hekmat ast
Az ghame roozegare doon tab-e sokhan gozaar koo

حافظ اگرچه در سخن خازن گنج حکمت است
از غم روزگار دون طبع سخن گزار کو

On account of the bow of your eyebrow blood pours from my eye,
On account of this eye and that eyebrow the world is in full cry.

I am slave to the eye of that Turk[1] that in intoxication is slumbering;
In the garden of that one's face, shade the musky eyebrow is providing.

From longing my body is a crescent moon; a musky, bow-shaped inscription;
To appear as an eyebrow in heaven, how can the moon have such aspiration?

The watcher is not cautious, for every moment from eye and eyebrow,
A thousand kinds of messages come, disguised by that one's eyebrow[2].

To the souls of those in seclusion, that brow is a garden of beauty,
On the border of the Jasmine patch, the eyebrow strolls grandly.

Such beauty! Now no one will talk about the Houri or the Pari[3],
Comparing the eye of one, or the eyebrow of the other, casually.

O you, with an unbelieving heart; you do not cover your hair;
I fear that your eyebrow may become the arch for my prayer.

Though Hafiz was a wily bird, who pressed his suit with great know-how,
He was struck by the arrow of your glance from the bow of your eyebrow.

(W-C 475) The radif here is "Eyebrow".
[1] "...Turk..." See glossary in volume one.
[2] This verse echoes words of Khawaja Muinuddin Hasan Chishti who says "Every moment the dervish receives hundreds of messages from the unseen world". See The Meditations of Khawaja Muinuddin Hasan Chishti (see bibliography in volume one).
[3] "...Houri...Pari..." See glossary in volume one.

Maraa chashmist khoon afshaan ze daste aan kamaan abroo
Jahaan por fetne khaahad shod az in chashmo azaan abroo

مرا چشمیست خون افشان ز دست آن کمان ابرو
جهان پر فتنه خواهد شد از این چشم و از آن ابرو

Gholaame chashme aan torkam ke dar khaabe khoshe masti
Negaarin golshanash rooyasto moshkin saaye baan abroo

غلام چشم آن ترکم که در خواب خوش مستی
نگارین گلشنش روی است و مشکین سایان ابرو

Helaali shod tanam zin gham ke baa toghraaye moshkinash
Ke baashad mah ke ben maayad ze taaghe aasmaan abroo

هلالی شد تنم زین غم که با طغرای مشکینش
که باشد مه که بنماید ز طاق آسمان ابرو

Raghibaan ghaafelo maa raa az aan chashmo jabin har dam
Hezaaraan goone peighaam asto haajeb dar miyaan abroo

رقیبان غافل و ما را از آن چشم و جبین هر دم
هزاران گونه پیغام است و حاجب در میان ابرو

Ravaane gooshe giraan raa jabinash torfe golzarist
Ke bar tarfe saman zaarash hami gardad chamaan abroo

روان گوشه گیران را جبینش طرفه گلزاریست
که بر طرف سمن زارش همی گردد چمان ابرو

Degar hooro pari raa kas nagooyad baa chonin hosni
Ke in raa in chonin chashm asto aanraa aan chonaan abroo

دگر حور و پری را کس نگوید با چنین حسنی
که این را این چنین چشم است و آن را آن چنان ابرو

To kaafar del nemibandi neghaabe zolfo mitarsam
Ke mehraabam begardaanad khame aan delsetaan abroo

تو کافر دل نمی بندی نقاب زلف و میترسم
که محرابم بگرداند خم آن دلستان ابرو

Agar che morghe zirak bood Hafez dar havaa daari
Be tire ghamze seydash kard chashme aan kamaan abroo

اگرچه مرغ زیرک بود حافظ در هواداری
به تیر غمزه صیدش کرد چشم آن کمان ابرو

Messenger of the true ones, say how the friend is,
Tell that balladeer, the bulbul, how the rose is.

To this poverty stricken one, tell about the wealthy,
Regale this beggar with the great king's story.

Don't grieve, for in the home of the fond we are treated fondly;
Of the friend's fondness tell the friend a fond story.

When the two tips of your musky hair touched in that way,
What meaning did it have for us? For the sake of God say.

If they say the dust of that one's way is not Kohl[1] for the eye,
Say to them that it is, and the evidence for it is in our eye.

Quick! To the door, the masters of wisdom come with their story,
Go, hear their mysteries; come back and tell the tale to me.

Last night my crying set the garden's bird a weeping,
Breeze, are you unaware of what passed? Start telling!

Should you pass again the door of fortune on your way,
After offering your service and making supplication, say –

"In love's path there is no distinction between rich and poor,
So, O great king of beauty, will you not speak to the poor?"

To the one who forbids our going to the tavern, say,
"Come and say to the Elder what it is you have to say".

The wine that, still in the jug, took away the heart of the Sufi,
O Saki, do say, when in the glass will it display its coquetry?

Hafiz, if to that one's gathering they grant you entry,
Drink wine, and for the sake of God eschew hypocrisy.

(W-C 476) The radif here is "Utters" or "Says".
  [1] *"..Kohl..." See glossary in volume one.*
  [2] *"..Elder..." See commentary to W-C 471 above.*

Ey peyke raastaan khabare yaare maa begoo
Ahvaale gol be bolbole dastaan saraa begoo

ای پیک راستان خبر یار ما بگو
احوال گل به بلبل دستان سرا بگو

Bar in faghir ghesseye aan moh tasham bekhaan
Baa in gedaa hekaayate aan paadshaa begoo

بر این فقیر قصّه آن محتشم بخوان
با این گدا حکایت آن پادشا بگو

Maa mahramaane khalvate onsim gham makhor
Baa yaare aashnaa sokhane aashnaa begoo

ما محرمان خلوت انسیم غم مخور
با یار آشنا سخن آشنا بگو

Bar ham cho mizad aan sare zolfeyne moshkbaar
Baa maa sare che daasht ze bahre khodaa begoo

بر هم چو می زد آن سر زلفین مشکبار
با ما سر چه داشت ز بهر خدا بگو

Har kas ke goft khaake rahe ou na tootiyaast
Goo in sokhan moaayene dar chashme maa begoo

هر کس که گفت خاک ره او نه توتیاست
گو این سخن معاینه در چشم ما بگو

Haan bar dar ast ghesseye arbaabe ma-refat
Ramzi boro bepors hadisi biyaa begoo

هان بر در است قصّه ارباب معرفت
رمزی برو بپرس حدیثی بیا بگو

Morghe chaman be mooyeye man doosh migerist
Aakher na vaaghefi ke che raft ey sabaa begoo

مرغ چمن به مویه من دوش می گریست
آخر نه واقفی که چه رفت ای صبا بگو

Gar digarat bar aan dare dovlat gozar bovad
Ba-d az adaaye khedmato arze doaa begoo

گر دیگرت بر آن در دولت گذر بود
بعد از ادای خدمت و عرض دعا بگو

Dar raahe eshgh farghe ghaniyyo faghir nist
Ey paad shaahe hosn sokhan baa gedaa begoo

در راه عشق فرق غنّی و فقیر نیست
ای پادشاه حسن سخن با گدا بگو

Aan kas ke man-e maa ze kharaabaat mikonad
Goo dar hozoore pire man in maajaraa begoo

آن کس که منع ما ز خرابات می کند
گو در حضور پیر من این ماجرا بگو

Aan mey ke dar saboo dele soofi be eshve bord
Key dar ghadah kereshme konad saaghiyaa begoo

آن می که در سبو دل صوفی به عشوه برد
کی در قدح کرشمه کند ساقیا بگو

Hafez garat be majlese ou raah midahand
Mey noosho tarke zargh ze bahre khodaa begoo

حافظ گرت به مجلس او راه میدهند
می نوش و ترک زرق ز بهر خدا بگو

The green[1] field of the sky and the new moon's sickle I observed,
What I had sown in my field and the time of reaping I recalled.

I said: "Fortune, the sun has risen, whilst you were slumbering!"
You said: "Don't despair of what once was, in spite of everything".

At death ascend to heaven as the Messiah has done,
So a hundred rays of light from your lamp may reach the sun[2].

To that night-stealing star[2], for support, it's better not to go,
It took the throne from Kay Kaus and the belt of Khusroe[3].

The ear may be weighed down with earrings of gold and ruby,
But hear my counsel; soon goes the time of youth and beauty.

May the evil eye be far from your mole, for on the chess board of beauty[4],
It moved just a pawn and took the prize from sun and moon completely.

Tell the revolving heavens not to boast too loudly, for in love's way,
The moon reaps one barley corn; for 'seven sisters',[5] only two they pay.

The fire of hypocritical piety will burn up religion's harvest,
Hafiz, to throw your Sufi coat away and go, would be best.

(W-C 477)

[1] "..Green field..." Literally this is 'green'. The sky is sometimes described thus by Hafiz but here the likening of the moon to a sickle makes it clear what he is intending.

[2] I take this verse to mean that, having overslept, rather than wasting time feeling bad about it – just get on and hope for the best. The equivalent of saying it was Allah's Will.

[3] "...Kay Kaus...Kay Khusroe..." Former or legendary kings.

[4] "...on the chess board of beauty..." In a previous ghazal Hafiz has used the image of the chessboard to imply the dimension of 'Haqiqat'. See verse 3, ghazal 24 (W-C 28).Though the term is not used by Hafiz in the previous ghazal it is clear the first lines refer, in ascending order, to what the Sufis call Shariat, Tariqat, Haqiqat and Ma'rifat.

[5] "...'seven sisters'..." The star formation known as the Pleiades.

Mazra e sabze falak didamo daase mahe nov

Yaadam az keshteye khish aamado hengaame derov

مزرع سبز فلک دیدم و داس مه نو

یادم از کشته خویش آمد و هنگام درو

Goftam ey bakht bekhosbidiyo khorshid damid

Goft baa in hame az saabeghe novmid mashov

گفتم ای بخت بخسبیدی و خورشید دمید

گفت با این همه از سابقه نومید مشو

Anchonaan rov shabe rehlat cho masihaa be falak

Kaz cheraaghe to be khorshid rasad sad partov

آنچنان رو شب رحلت چو مسیحا به فلک

کز چراغ تو به خورشید رسد صد پرتو

Tekye bar akhtare shab dozd makon kin ayyaar

Takhte kavoos bebordo kamare key khosrov

تکیه بر اختر شب دزد مکن کاین عیّار

تخت کاووس ببرد و کمر کیخسرو

Gooshvaare zar o la-l arche geraan daarad goosh

Dovre khoobi gozaraan ast nasihat beshenov

گوشوار زر و لعل ارچه گران دارد گوش

دور خوبی گذران است نصیحت بشنو

Chashme bad door ze khaale to ke dar arseye hosn

Beydaghi raand ke bord az maho khorshid gerov

چشم بد دور ز خال تو که در عرصه حسن

بیدقی راند که برد از مه و خورشید گرو

Aas maan goo maforoosh in azamat kandar eshgh

Kharmane mah be jovi khoosheye parvin be do jov

آسمان گو مفروش این عظمت کاندر عشق

خرمن مه به جوی خوشه پروین به دو جو

Aatashe zohde riyaa kharmane din khaahad sookht

Hafez in khergheye pashmine biyandaazo boro

آتش زهد ریا خرمن دین خواهد سوخت

حافظ این خرقه پشمینه بینداز و برو

The beloved said, "The spectacle of the new moon you went out to see,
Go then! Before my moon-shaped eyebrow ashamed you should be"[1].

"Since our hair made captive your heart a lifetime it seems to be,
"Do not be careless; toward friends behave more considerately.

"Don't sell the scent of intelligence for our Hindu-dark hair,
A thousand musk pods fetch only half a barley corn there."

The seed of love and fidelity in this old garden nursery,
When the time for harvesting arrives, is seen manifestly.

Saki, bring wine, so that I can tell you of the mystery,
Of the ancient star's travels and the new moon's journey.

At the month's end the waning moon's crescent points to,
Siyamak's long gone diadem and the end of the crown of Zhu[2].

Hafiz, the Magian Pir's doorstep is the shelter for fidelity,
Hear what he says when you read the lesson of love's story.

(W-C 478)

[1] The implication of verse one appears to be that the beloved is scolding the lover for preferring the attraction of the outward to the beloved's concealed beauty.
[2] "...Siyamak... Zhu..." Legendary ancient rulers of Persia. The point here may, following the previous verse, relate to the transitory nature of earthly sovereignty. A deeper level of meaning can also potentially be inferred from the entire ghazal concerning the inner and outer nature of astrology.

Goftaa boroon shodi be tamaashaaye maahe nov
Az maahe abrovaane manat sharm baad rov

گفتا برون شدی به تماشای ماه نو
از ماه ابروان منت شرم باد رو

Omrist taa delat ze asiraane zolfe maast
Ghaafel ze hefze jaanebe yaaraane khod mashov

عمریست تا دلت ز اسیران زلف ماست
غافل ز حفظ جانب یاران خود مشو

Mafroosh atre aghl be hendooye zolfe maa
Kaanjaa hezaar naafeye moshkin be nim jov

مفروش عطر عقل به هندوی زلف ما
کانجا هزار نافه مشکین به نیم جو

Tokhme vafaavo mehr dar in kohne kesht zaar
Aangah ayaan shavad ke rasad movseme derov

تخم وفا و مهر دراین کهنه کشت‌ه زار
آنگه عیان شود که رسد موسم درو

Saaghi biyaar baade ke ramzi begooyamat
Az serre akhtaraane kohan seyro maahe nov

ساقی بیار باده که رمزی بگویمت
از سرّ اختران کهن سیر و ماه نو

Shekle helaale har sare mah midahad neshaan
Az afsare siyaamako tarke kolaahe zov

شکل هلال هر سر مه میدهد نشان
از افسر سیامک و ترک کلاه زو

Hafez jenaab pire moghaan ma-mane vafaast
Darse hadise eshgh bar ou khaan vazoo shenov

حافظ جناب پیر مغان مأمن وفاست
درس حدیث عشق بر او خوان و زو شنو

O you who have come with a lock of hair, long and trailing,
The one who is crazy may you find some time to be treating.

For a moment leave your customary coquettish disdaining,
Since it is after the masters of need you have come inquiring.

Whether in peace or in war, your stature I die before,
For your flirtatious ways become you well for sure.

In your ruby lip fire and water are blended amazingly,
Near such a fine magician may the evil eye never be.

May goodness be on your tender heart, because for the reward's sake,
You come to read the last rites over one whose life your look did take.

What's my piety worth when, so my heart you can be plundering,
You have come to the sanctuary of my secret[1], drunk and raving.

"O Hafiz!" he said, "Your robe is stained with wine yet again,
From the rites of that religious order have you come back again?"

(W-C 479) The radif here is "You have come."
 [1] "...secret..." a possible reference to the purified heart also known as the Secret.

Ey ke baa sel seleye zolfe deraaz aamade ee
Forsatat baad ke divaane navaaz aamade ee

ای که با سلسله زلف دراز آمده ای
فرصتت باد که دیوانه نواز آمده ای

Saa-ati naaz mafarmaayo begardaan aadat
Chon be porsidane arbaabe niyaaz aamade ee

ساعتی ناز مفرمای و بگردان عادت
چون به پرسیدن ارباب نیاز آمده ای

Pishe baalaaye to naazam che be solho che be jang
Ke be har haal baraa zandeye naaz aamade ee

پیش بالای تو نازم چه به صلح و چه به جنگ
که به هر حال براندازنده ناز آمده ای

Aabo aatash be ham aamikhte ee az labe la-l
Chashme bad door ke khosh shobade baaz aamade ee

آب و آتش بهم آمیخته ای از لب لعل
چشم بد دور که خوش شعبده باز آمده ای

Aafarin bar dele narme to ke az bahre savaab
Koshteye ghamzeye khod raa be namaaz aamade ee

آفرین بر دل نرم تو که از بهر ثواب
کشته غمزه خود را به نماز آمده ای

Zohde man baa to che sanjad ke be yaghmaaye delam
Masto aashofte be khalvat gahe raaz aamade ee

زهد من با تو چه سنجد که به یغمای دلم
مست و آشفته به خلوتگه راز آمده ای

Goft Hafez degarat kherghe sharaab aaloodast
Magar az mazhabe in taayefe baaz aamade ee

گفت حافظ دگرت خرقه شراب آلوده ست
مگر از مذهب این طایفه باز آمده ای

* این غزل بر اساس شماره گذاری کلارک در میان غزلهای حرف «ه» آمده است.

With the boiling blood of my heart I wrote a letter to the friend,
Saying "In separation the torment of the Judgement I apprehend".

My eyes show a hundred signs of separation's agony,
These tears from my eyes are not the only signs surely!

I put that one to the test and derived no benefit,
One who tests the tested will rue that he did it.

I asked of a doctor about what the state of the friend might be,
He said, "In distance is torment, in proximity there is security."

If I roam your street blame will fall on me,
By Allah, in love this happens inevitably.

Now Hafiz is a seeker, for his sweet life give a cup,
So the taste of beneficence he may find in the cup.

(W-C 480) This ghazal according to W-C is in a style called called 'Mulama' – consisting of alternate lines in Arabic and Farsi.

Az sooze del neveshtam nazdike doost naama

Enni ra ayto dahran men hejrekal ghiyaama

از سوز دل نوشتم نزدیک دوست نامه

انّی رایت دهراً من هجرک القیامه

Daaram man az feraaghash dar dide sad alaamat

Lay sat domoo o ayni haazaa lanal alaama

دارم من از فراقش در دیده صد علامت

لیست دموع عینی هذا لنا العلامه

Har chand kaaz moodam az vey nabood soodam

Man jarrabal mojarrab hallat behen nadaama

هرچند کازمودم از وی نبود سودم

من جرّب المجرّب حلّت به النّدامه

Porsidam az tabibi ahvaale doost goftaa

Fi bo dehaa azaabon fi ghorbehas salaama

پرسیدم از طبیبی احوال دوست گفتا

فی بعدها عذاب فی قربها السّلامه

Goftam malaamat aayad gar gerde koot gardam

Vallaah maa ra aynaa hobban belaa malaama

گفتم ملامت آید گر گرد کوت گردم

والله ما راینا حبّا بلا ملامه

Hafez cho taaleb aamad jaami be jaane shirin

Hattaa yazoogho menho ka san menal keraama

حافظ چو طالب آمد جامی به جان شیرین

حتّی یذوق منه کأسا من الکرامه

You are the light of my eye, O beloved; from me do not be apart,
My very life's beloved you are, and friend of the affrighted heart.

The lovers will not let go your garment,
The shirt of their patience you have rent.

May the eye of good fortune avert harm from you,
For perfection in heart stealing is surpassed by you.

O cleric of our time you forbid that one's love to me?
You are excused because that one you did not see.

The criticism that the friend has made of you, Hafiz,
Could it be beyond the cover of your rug your foot is.[1]

(W-C 481) The radif here is "You have attained", or "You have seen" & etc.
[1] *"..beyond the cover..." This implies the speaker may have said more than he should.*
(W-C 482) See appendix.

Az man jodaa mashov ke toam noore dide ee

Mahboobe jaano moonese ghalbe ramide ee

از من جدا مشو که توأم نور دیده ای

محبوب جان و مونس قلب رمیده ای

Az daamane to dast nadaarand aasheghaan

Piraahane sabooriye ishaan deride ee

از دامن تو دست ندارند عاشقان

پیراهن صبوری ایشان دریده ای

Az chashme bakhte khish mabaadat gazand azaank

Dar delbari be ghaayate khoobi raside ee

از چشم بخت خویش مبادت گزند از آنک

در دلبری به غایت خوبی رسیده ای

Man-am koni ze eshghe vey ey moftiye zamaan

Ma zoor daaramat ke to ou raa nadide ee

منعم کنی ز عشق وی ای مفتی زمان

معذور دارمت که تو او را ندیده ای

Aan sarzanesh ke kard to raa doost Hafezaa

Bish az gelime khish magar paa keshide ee

آن سرزنش که کرد ترا دوست حافظا

بیش از گلیم خویش مگر پا کشیده ای

Happy amber-scented breeze, a sweet the heart is desiring,
That in longing for you at the crack of dawn it was arising.

O you bird with such a fortunate look, on the Way guide me,
In longing for the dust of your door my eye became watery.

To recall my thin wasted form, that in the heart's blood is immersed,
The new moon's crescent in the red glow of twilight can be observed.

It is I breathing without you! O what a shame there is on me!
Perhaps you'll forgive; for such a sin what excuse can there be?

From your company, on love's path, dawn was learning,
How to shred the black vest underneath the clothing.

Due to my love for you, when from this world I will go,
Not wild weeds, but the red rose from my grave will grow.

By tiredness with me don't let your tender heart so soon be affected,
The opening words[1], "In God's Name" your Hafiz has only now said.

(W-C 483)

[1] "...The opening words..." These are "Bismillah ar Rehmanir Raheem" in Arabic, and are used before
commencing any activity. The implication here is that it is only on dying that Hafiz's heart has uttered these
words. In other words death is seen as a beginning.

Khonok nasime moambar shamaameye del khaah
Ke dar havaaye to bar khaast baamdaade pegaah

خنک نسیم معنبر شمامه دلخواه
که در هوای تو برخاست بامداد پگاه

Dalile raah sho ey taayere khojaste leghaa
Ke dide aab shod az shovghe khaake aan dar gaah

دلیل راه شو ای طایر خجسته لقا
که دیده آب شد از شوق خاک آن درگاه

Be yaade shakhse nazaaram ke gharghe khoone delast
Helaal raa be kenaare shafagh konid negaah

به یاد شخص نزارم که غرق خون دل است
هلال را به کنار شفق کنید نگاه

Manam ke bi to nafas mizanam zehi khejlat
Magar to afv koni var na nist ozre gonaah

منم که بی تو نفس می زنم زهی خجلت
مگر تو عفو کنی ورنه نیست عذر گناه

Ze doostaane to aamookht dar tarighate mehr
Sepide dam ke havaa chaak zad she aare siyaah

ز دوستان تو آموخت در طریقت مهر
سپیده دم که هوا چاک زد شعار سیاه

Be eshghe rooye to roozi ke az jahaan beravam
Ze torbatam bedamad sorkh gol be jaaye giyaah

به عشق روی تو روزی که از جهان بروم
ز تربتم بدمد سرخ گل به جای گیاه

Made be khaatere naazok malaalat az man zood
Ke Hafeze to khod in lahze goft besmellaah

مده به خاطر نازک ملالت از من زود
که حافظ تو خود این لحظه گفت بسم الله

Swept, and with water cleaned, the door of the Magian's house was,
Sitting there, welcoming the old and young that venerable one was.

Girded were the loins of every wine-drinker and servant to serve him,
But by the crown of his hat the canopy of clouds were covered up by him[1].

The brightness of the goblet and cup encompassed the moon's light,
The beaming faces of the Magian's children outshone the sun's light.

Though having a thousand charms, Fortune in the bridal chamber,
Curled again her locks of hair and on rose petals sprinkled rose water.

Due to the joyful cries of the young ones of beautiful temperament,
Sugar lost its value, jasmine petals fell, and the Rebab was silent.

I made my salaam; and that one spoke with face smiling,
"O you poor one, hung-over from all your wine drinking,

"Who, however foolish, like you would be acting,
"Leaving the treasure house and in a ruin camping?

"I fear union with a Wakeful Fortune they won't be giving,
"For Sleeping fortune, in sleep you have been embracing.

"The entire sphere is the horse-groom of Nusratuddin[2],
"Come, for an angel holding his stirrup can be seen.

"The intellect inspired by the Unseen, to acquire its own dignity,
"From the ninth heaven blows a hundred kisses toward his majesty.

"Come to the tavern Hafiz, so that there you'll be presented,
With a thousand rows of prayers that were all accepted."

(W-C 484) The radif here varies in translation; "Gave" "Fixed" & etc.
[1] Verse two has been translated by Saberi to mean that the servants felt so honoured that their heads touched the clouds. We have taken it to mean that the wine drinkers covered their loins to serve; but his hat is like a crown that girds the heavens. This seems o be supported by the following verse with its 'cosmic' references. The first five verses all appear to glorify the Magian Pir and his 'children' or qualities. The latter part of the ghazal consists of the advice given by the Magian Pir.
[2] "...Nusratuddin..." An ally of Hafiz's patron, who may well have been in the ascendant politically at that time. See Avery's notes; pp. 370.

Dare saraaye moghaan rofte boodo aab zade
Neshaste piro salaaee be sheykho shaab zade

در سرای مغان رفته بود و آب زده
نشسته پیر و صلایی به شیخ و شاب زده

Saboo keshaan hame dar bandegish baste kamar
Vali ze tarke kolah chatr bar sahaab zade

سبوکشان همه در بندگیش بسته کمر
ولی ز ترک کله چتر بر سحاب زده

Shoaa e jaamo ghadah noore maah pooshide
Ezaare mogh bachegaan raahe aaftaab zade

شعاع جام و قدح نور ماه پوشیده
عذار مغبچگان راه آفتاب زده

Aroose bakht dar aan hejle baa hezaaraan naaz
Shekaste kasmevo bar barge gol golaab zade

عروس بخت در آن حجله با هزاران ناز
شکسته کسمه و بر برگ گل گلاب زده

Ze shooro arbadeye shaahedaane shirin kaar
Shekar shekaste saman rikhte robaab zade

ز شور و عربده شاهدان شیرین کار
شکر شکسته سمن ریخته رباب زده

Salaam kardamo baa man be rooye khandaan goft
Ke ey khomaar kashe moflese sharaab zade

سلام کردم و با من به روی خندان گفت
که ای خمار کش مفلس شراب زده

Ke in konad ke to kardi be za-fe hemmato raay
Ze ganj khaane shode kheyme bar kharaab zade

که این کند که تو کردی به ضعف همّت و رای
ز گنج خانه شده خیمه بر خراب زده

Vesaale dovlate bidaar tarsamat nadahand
Che khoftei to dar aaghooshe bakhte khaab zade

وصال دولت بیدار ترسمت ندهند
چو خفته ای تو در آغوش بخت خواب زده

Falak janibe kashe shaah nosrateddin ast
Biyaa bebin malakash dast dar rekaab zade

فلک جنیبه کش شاه نصرت الدّین است
بیا ببین ملکش دست در رکاب زده

Kherad ke molheme gheyb ast bahre kasbe sharaf
Ze baame arsh sadash boose bar jenaab zade

خرد که ملهم غیب است بهر کسب شرف
ز بام عرش صدش بوسه بر جناب زده

Biyaa be meykade Hafez ke bar to arze konam
Hezaar saf ze doaa haaye mostajaab zade

بیا به میکده حافظ که بر تو عرضه کنم
هزار صف ز دعاهای مستجاب زده

Last night I went to the door of the tavern, sleep stained,
My robe was wet and the prayer mat was wine stained.

The Magian child of the wine vendor came chaffing me,
Saying "Wake up you traveller for stained with sleep you be!

"Cleanse yourself thoroughly then come to the tavern happily,
"For this house of the ruined ones stained by you must not be!

"In desire for lips of sweet boys how long will you be,
"Staining the essence of the soul with liquefied ruby.

"Live out the stage of your later years with pure chastity,
"Don't stain age's robe as you did youths, with folly.

"Those who know love's way, in its deep sea,
"Drowned, but from its water emerged stain free.

"From the well of your nature emerge, clean and with purity,
For from water mixed with mud you will not gain purity".

I said, "O life and soul of the world, don't be worrying,
If the rose's book is stained by pure wine in the spring."

He said, "Hafiz, don't sell friends such points of subtle sophistry!"
What a pity! So much charm stained with such a critical tendency.

(W-C 485) The radif here is "Stained"

Doosh raftam be dare meykade khaab aaloode
Kherghe tar daamano sajjaade sharaab aaloode

دوش رفتم به در میکده خواب آلوده
خرقه تر دامن و سجّاده شراب آلوده

Aamad afsoos konaan mogh bacheye baade foroosh
Goft bidaar sho ey rahrove khaab aaloode

آمد افسوس کنان مغبچه باده فروش
گفت بیدار شو ای رهرو خواب آلوده

Shosto shooee bekon aangah be kharaabaat kharaam
Taa nagardad ze to in deyre kharaab aaloode

شست و شوئی بکن آنگه به خرابات خرام
تا نگردد ز تو این دیر خراب آلوده

Dar havaaye labe shirin pesaraan chand koni
Jovhare rooh be yaaghoote mozaab aaloode

در هوای لب شیرین پسران چند کنی
جوهر روح به یاقوت مذاب آلوده

Be tahaarat gozaraan manzele piriyyo makon
Khel-ate sheyb cho tashrife shabaab aaloode

به طهارت گذران منزل پیریّ و مکن
خلعت شیب چون تشریف شباب آلوده

Aashnaayaane rahe eshgh darin bahre ameegh
Gharghe gashtando nagashtand be aab aaloode

آشنایان ره عشق درین بحر عمیق
غرقه گشتند و نگشتند به آب آلوده

Paako saafi shovo az chaahe tabiat be dar aay
Ke safaaee nadahad aabe toraab aaloode

پاک و صافی شو و از چاه طبیعت به در آی
که صفائی ندهد آب تراب آلوده

Goftam ey jaane jahaan daftare gol eybi nist
Ke shavad fasle bahaar az meye naab aaloode

گفتم ای جان جهان دفتر گل عیبی نیست
که شود فصل بهار از می ناب آلوده

Goft Hafez loghozo nokte be yaaraan maforoosh
Aah azin lotfe be an-vaae etaab aaloode

گفت حافظ لغز و نکته به یاران مفروش
آه ازین لطف به انواع عتاب آلوده

Drawing back the gold embroidered robe that one passed on disdainfully,
A hundred moon-faced beauties ripped their brocaded collars enviously.

From the wine-heating fire that one's face with sweat dripped,
Like beads of night dew that on to the rose petal has dropped.

Born from the water of grace, that one's life giving ruby;
That statuesque box-tree saunter, nurtured with delicacy.

Sweet of locution, tall and with an elegant fine motion,
A heart catching face with almond eyes for attraction.

See the heart seducing ruby lip, hear laughter that's heart killing,
See the grace filled movements in the slow measured walking.

From our snare, that black eyed deer has simply departed,
Friends, how to manage the state of my heart, so desolated.

Take care, as much as possible, not to hurt the ones who can see,
O, my chosen companion, this changing world has no fidelity.

Your heart-deceiving look, how long to bear its tyranny,
Light of my two eyes, one day send an inviting glance to me.

If Hafiz has said something to cause hurt to your heart's nobility,
Come back, for what we said and heard we have repented fully.

(W-C 486) The radif here varies in translation; "Torn"; "Dropped"; "Drawn" & etc.

Daaman keshaan hami shod dar shorbe zar keshide
Sad maah roo ze rashkash jeybe ghasab deride

دامن کشان همی شد در شرب زر کشیده
صد ماهرو ز رشکش جیب قصب دریده

Az taabe aatashe mey bar gerde aarezash khey
Chon ghatrehaaye shabnam bar barge gol chekide

از تاب آتش می بر گرد عارضش خوی
چون قطره های شبنم بر برگ گل چکیده

Yaaghoote jaan fazaayash az aabe lotf zaade
Shemshaade khosh kharaamash dar naaz parvaride

یاقوت جان فزایش از آب لطف زاده
شمشاد خوش خرامش در ناز پروریده

Lafzi fasih shirin ghaddi boland chaabok
Rooee latif delkash chashmi khoshe keshide

لفظی فصیح شیرین قدّی بلند چابک
روئی لطیف دلکش چشمی خوش کشیده

Aan la-le delkashash bin vaan khandeye del aashoob
Vaan raftane khoshash bin vaan gaame aaramide

آن لعل دلکشش بین وان خنده دل آشوب
وان رفتن خوشش بین وان گام آرمیده

Aan aahooye siyah chashm az daame maa boroon shod
Yaaraan che chaare saazim baa in dele ramide

آن آهوی سیه چشم از دام ما برون شد
یاران چه چاره سازیم با این دل رمیده

Zenhaar taa tavaani ahle nazar mayaazaar
Donyaa vafaa nadaarad ey yaare bar gozide

زنهار تا توانی اهل نظر میازار
دنیا وفا ندارد ای یار برگزیده

Taa key kasham atibat az chashme del faribat
Roozi kereshme eek on ey noore har do dide

تا کی کشم عتیبت ازچشم دلفریبت
روزی کرشمه ای کن ای نور هر دو دیده

Gar khaatere sharifat ranjide shod ze Hafez
Baaz aa ke tovbe kardim az goftevo shanide

گر خاطر شریفت رنجیده شد ز حافظ
بازآ که توبه کردیم از گفته و شنیده

By last night's wine still drunk, in the early morning,
I took the wine cup with harp and Chagane[1] playing.

I made ready provisions of wine for reason's travelling,
And from the city of self-existence I sent him packing.

Such an arch look my wine-selling beauty threw me,
That from the trickery that time uses I found safety.

From the Saki with bow-like eyebrow I was hearing,
"O you, whom the arrow of reproach is hitting,

"Like the sash, from the waist you get nothing,
"If all you see there is your own self existing.

"Go as you wish; for another bird set this snare,
For the Anqa's[2] nest is very high above there."

The musician, close friend and the Saki are one really,
Water and clay that seem to intervene are imaginary.

Supply the wine ship so that we may happily,
Pass over this ocean without any boundary.

Our existence is a complete enigma, O Hafiz,
In trying to solve it only fable and folly there is.

(W-C 487)
  [1] "...Chagane A four stringed instrument
  [2] "...Anqa..." See glossary in volume one.

Sahar gaahaan ke makhmoore shabaane
Gereftam baade baa chango chaghaane
سحرگاهان که مخمور شبانه
گرفتم باده با چنگ و چغانه

Nahaadam aghl raa rah tooshe az mey
Ze shahre hastiyash kardam ravaane
نهادم عقل را ره توشه از می
ز شهر هستی اش کردم روانه

Negaare mey foroosham eshvei daad
Ke eemen gashtam az makre zamaane
نگار می فروشم عشوه ای داد
که ایمن گشتم از مکر زمانه

Ze saaghiye kamaan abroo shanidam
Ke ey tire malaamat raa neshaane
ز ساقیّ کمان ابرو شنیدم
که ای تیر ملامت را نشانه

Nabandi zaan miyaan tarfi kamar vaar
Agar khod raa bebini dar miyaane
نبندی زان میان طرفی کمر وار
اگر خود را ببینی در میانه

Boro in daam bar morghi degar neh
Ke anghaa raa boland ast aashiyaane
برو این دام بر مرغی دگر نه
که عنقا را بلند است آشیانه

Nadimo motrebo saaghi hame oust
Khiyaale aabo gel dar rah bahaane
ندیم و مطرب و ساقی همه اوست
خیال آب و گل در ره بهانه

Bede kashtiye may taa khosh bar aaeem
Azin daryaaye naa peydaa karaane
بده کشتی می تا خوش برآئیم
از این دریای ناپیدا کرانه

Vojoode maa moammaaist Hafez
Ke tahghighash fosoon asto fasaane
وجود ما معمّائیست حافظ
که تحقیقش فسونست و فسانه

The candle was made a moth by the shining lamp of your face,
Due to your mole[1], for interest in myself I have found no place.

Reason, that once kept in chains the love-crazy,
From the scent of your hair lost its own sanity.

The candle gladly gave its life to the breeze the very moment,
That it got a message that the candle of your face had sent.

What if the wind takes life due to carrying the scent of you?
To the beloved the sacrifice of a thousand dear souls is due.

To burn on the fire of that beautiful face instead of rue seed[2],
Other than the beloved's mole what better could we need?

Last night I was swept off my feet by jealousy,
When with a stranger my beloved I could see.

What stratagems we devised but to no avail,
Our cunning, with that one, became a fairy tale.

I made a pact with the round lip of the friend of mine,
So my tongue tells no tale except of the cup of wine.

Stories of the College and Sufi Khanqah[3] don't be reciting,
For into Hafiz's head the desire for the tavern is falling.

(W-C 488)

[1] *"...mole..." See glossary in volume one.*
[2] *"...rue seed..." See glossary in volume one.*
[3] *"...Sufi Khanqah..." The place where the Sufis carry out their rituals, such as Zikr and meditation.*

Cheraaghe rooye to raa sha-m gasht parvaane

Maraa ze khaale to baa haale khish parvaa ne

چراغ روی ترا شمع گشت پروانه

مرا ز خال تو با حال خویش پروا نه

Kherad ke gheyde majaanine eshgh mi farmood

Be booye halgheye zolfe to gasht divaane

خرد که قید مجانین عشق می فرمود

به بوی حلقه زلف تو گشت دیوانه

Be mojde jaan be sabaa daad sha-m dar nafasi

Ze sham-e rooye toash chon rasid parvaane

به مژده جان به صبا داد شمع در نفسی

ز شمع روی توأش چون رسید پروانه

Be booye zolfe to gar jaan be baad raft che shod

Hezaar jaane geraami fadaaye jaanaane

به بوی زلف تو گر جان به باد رفت چه شد

هزار جان گرامی فدای جانانه

Bar aatashe rokhe zibaaye ou be jaaye sepand

Be gheyre khaale siyaahash ke did beh daane

برآتش رخ زیبای او به جای سپند

به غیر خال سیاهش که دید به دانه

Mane ramide ze gheyrat ze paa fetaadam doosh

Negaare khish cho didam be daste bigaane

من رمیده ز غیرت ز پا فتادم دوش

نگار خویش چو دیدم به دست بیگانه

Che naghshhaa ke baran gikhtimo sood nadaasht

Fosoone maa bare ou gashte ast afsaane

چه نقشها که برانگیختیم و سود نداشت

فسون ما بر او گشته است افسانه

Maraa be dovre labe doost hast peymaani

Ke bar zabaan nabaram joz hadise peymaane

مرا به دور لب دوست هست پیمانی

که بر زبان نبرم جز حدیث پیمانه

Hadise madresevo khaan ghah magooy ke baaz

Fetaad dar sare Hafez havaaye mey khaane

حدیث مدرسه و خانقه مگوی که باز

فتاد در سر حافظ هوای میخانه

My heart's desiring of ruby wine is joy unending,
God be praised my work corresponds to my longing.

O you incalcitrant fortune, embrace that one tightly,
Now drink from the gold cup; now from the heart-loving lip of ruby.

To us, notoriety they have given, for our Rendi[1] way,
The ignorant elders and Sheykhs who've gone astray.

For the work of ascetic piety we have repented fully,
We seek God's forgiveness for being a ritual devotee.

My beloved to you separation's story how shall I reprise,
One eye - a hundred tears; one soul - a hundred sighs.

May no unbeliever feel even a trace of the pain, however slight,
That the moon does from your face; the cypress from your height.

In desire for your lip, from Hafiz's mind everything has gone;
Both the nightly reading and the early morning recitation.

(W-C 489)
[1] *"...Rendi..." Pertaining to profligacy.*

Eysham modaam ast az la-le del khaah
Kaaram be kaam ast al hamdo lelaah

عیشم مدام است از لعل دلخواه
کارم به کام است الحمدلله

Ey bakhte sarkash tangash be bar kash
Gah jaame zar kash gah la-le del khaah

ای بخت سرکش تنگش به برکش
گه جام زر کش گه لعل دلخواه

Maa raa be rendi afsaane kardand
Piraane jaahel sheykhaane gomraah

ما را به رندی افسانه کردند
پیران جاهل شیخان گمراه

Az daste zaahed kardim tovbe
Vaz fe-le aabed astaghforellah

از دست زاهد کردیم توبه
وز فعل عابد استغفرلله

Jaanaa che gooyam sharhe feraaghat
Chashmiyo sad nam janiyo sad aah

جانا چه گویم شرح فراقت
چشمیّ و صد نم جانی و صد آه

Kaafer mabinaad in gham ke didast
Az ghaamatat sarv az aarezat maah

کافر مبیناد این غم که دیده ست
از قامتت سرو از عارضت ماه

Shovghe labat bord az yade Hafez
Darse shabaane verde sahar gaah

شوق لبت برد از یاد حافظ
درس شبانه ورد سحرگاه

If in the street of that moon the sword rains many a blow,
Our neck we offer to it for God has surely decreed it so.

The rules governing piety we are aware of too,
But for our fortune gone awry what can we do?

I, a Rend and a lover – yet repenting?
God be forgiving, God be forgiving!

We don't care to hear the sheikh or preacher,
Either give us wine or make the story shorter[1].

Patience is something bitter, life passes quickly,
Wish I knew how long until with you I will be.

The sun-face of love is not reflected in our heart,
Oh mirror-face! This sigh is from your heart.

Hafiz, why complain? If you crave for union,
You must drink blood in and out of season.

(W-C 490)
  [1] *"...make the story shorter..." In other words – shorten the sermon.*
(W-C 491) See appendix.
(W-C 492) See appendix.

Gar tigh baarad dar kooye aan maah

Gardan nahaadim al hokmo lellaah

Aaeene taghvaa maa niz daanim

Liken che chaare baa bakhte gom raah

Man rendo aashegh vaan gaah tovbe

Astagh forellah astagh forellah

Maa sheykho vaaez kamtar shenaasim

Yaa jaame baade yaa ghesse kootaah

As sabro morron val omro fanen

Yaa layta sheri hattamo alghaah

Mehre to aksi bar maa nayafkand

Aaeene rooyaa aah az delat aah

Hafez che naali gar vasl khaahi

Khoon bayadat khord dar gaaho bigaah

گر تیغ بارد در کوی آن ماه

گردن نهادیم الحکم لله

آیین تقوی ما نیز دانیم

لیکن چه چاره با بخت گمراه

من رند و عاشق وانگاه توبه

استغفرلله استغفرلله

ما شیخ و واعظ کمتر شناسیم

یا جام باده یا قصّه کوتاه

الصّبر مرّ و العمر فان

یا لیت شعری حتّام القاه

مهر تو عکسی بر ما نیفکند

آیینه رویا آه از دلت آه

حافظ چه نالی گر وصل خواهی

خون بایدت خورد در گاه و بیگاه

Suddenly you have tossed aside the veil – what is all this?
Drunkenly you left the house – what's the meaning of this?

Your hair given to the breeze, your ear tuned to the rival is,
So with whatever comes you are agreeing? What means this?

Beggars favour you and king of the fair ones your status is,
You have not understood the rank you have, what is this?

Your hair into my hand you put first – didn't you do this?
Now you have knocked me off my feet – what is all this?

Your mouth's mystery, words hinted at; shown by belt the waist's secret is,
Yet you drew your sword from it in opposition – what means all this?

You rolled love's dice and engaged everyone in this,
You cheated them all in the end – what means this?

Hafiz, the beloved descended to your heart, that hurting is,
Yet you still hadn't got rid of the strangers – what means this?

(W-C 493) The radif here is "This is what?""We have used "What is this".

Naagahaan parde barandaakhtei ya-ni che
Mast az khaane boroon taakhtei ya-ni che

Zolf dar daste sabaa goosh be farmaane raghib
In chonin baa hame dar saakhtei ya-ni che

Shaahe khoobaaniyo manzoore gedaayaan shodei
Ghadre in martabe nashnaakhtei ya-ni che

Na sare zolfe khod avval to be dastam daadi
Baazam az paay darandaakhtei ya-ni che

Sokhanat ramze dahaan gofto kamar serre miyaan
Dar miyaan tigh be maa aakhtei ya-ni che

Har kas az mohreye mehre to be naghshi mashghool
Aaghebat baa hame kaj baakhtei ya-ni che

Hafezaa dar dele tangat cho forood aamad yaar
Khaane az gheyr napar daakhtei ya-ni che

ناگهان پرده برانداخته ای یعنی چه
مست از خانه برون تاخته ای یعنی چه

زلف در دست صبا گوش به فرمان رقیب
این چنین با همه درساخته ای یعنی چه

شاه خوبانی و منظور گدایان شده ای
قدر این مرتبه نشناخته ای یعنی چه

نه سرزلف خود اوّل تو به دستم دادی
بازم از پای درانداخته ای یعنی چه

سخنت رمز دهان گفت و کمر سرّ میان
در میان تیغ به ما آخته ای یعنی چه

هر کس از مهره مهر تو به نقشی مشغول
عاقبت با همه کج باخته ای یعنی چه

حافظا در دل تنگت چو فرود آمد یار
خانه از غیر نپرداخته ای یعنی چه

Compared to eternal life, your union is best,
O Lord, I pray give to me that which is best.

I told no one when with a sword you struck me,
The friend's secret is best hid from the enemy.

One night you said, "No one has ever seen anything,
In the whole world, better than my pearl earing".

Heart, in that one's street be a constant beggar,
Because that fortune is best that lasts forever.[1]

O pious man to paradise don't you go inviting me in,
Better than an orchard is this apple of that one's chin.

To die as a branded slave at your door is better,
On your life I swear, than all the world can offer.

The rose that gave up its life for the cypress tree,
Its dust is better than the blood of the arghavan tree.

For the sake of God, of my doctor make inquiry,
Ask when this disempowered one better will be.

Youth, from the counsel of the sage don't turn your head,
For better than youth's treasure is what the wise one said.

Every word in the mouth of the friend, a gem is,
But even better are utterances that come from Hafiz.

(W-C 494) The radif here is "Best" or "Better".
  [1] That fortune which is better than anything is of course the Love of God, which has no end.

Vesaale ou ze omre jaavdaan beh
Khodaavandaa maraa aan deh ke aan beh

وصال او ز عمر جاودان به
خداوندا مرا آن ده که آن به

Be shamshiram zado baa kas nagoftam
Ke raaze doost az doshman nahaan beh

به شمشیرم زد و با کس نگفتم
که راز دوست از دشمن نهان به

Shabi migoft chashme kas nadidast
Ze morvaaride goosham dar jahaan beh

شبی می گفت چشم کس ندیدست
ز مروارید گوشم در جهان به

Delaa daaem gedaaye kooye ou baash
Be hokme aanke dovlat jaavdaan beh

دلا دایم گدای کوی او باش
به حکم آنکه دولت جاودان به

Be kholdam da-vat ey zaahed mafarmaay
Ke in sibe zanakh zaan boostaan beh

به خلدم دعوت ای زاهد مفرمای
که این سیب زنخ زان بوستان به

Be daaghe bandegi mordan dar in dar
Be jaane ou ke az molke jahaan beh

به داغ بندگی مردن درین در
به جان او که از ملک جهان به

Goli kaan pay maale sarve maa gasht
Bovad khaakash ze khoone arghavaan beh

گلی کان پایمال سرو ما گشت
بود خاکش ز خون ارغوان به

Khodaa raa az tabibe man beporsid
Ke aakher key shavad in naatavaan beh

خدا را از طبیب من بپرسید
که آخر کی شود این ناتوان به

Javaanaa sar mataab az pande piraan
Ke raaye pir az bakhte javaan beh

جوانا سر متاب از پند پیران
که رای پیر از بخت جوان به

Sokhan andar dahaane doost govhar
Valikan gofteye Hafez az aan beh

سخن اندر دهان دوست گوهر
ولیکن گفته حافظ از آن به

O heart, passing through the street of love you don't do,
You have everything you need but this you do not do.

Desire's chaugan[1] is in your hand, but the ball you don't hit,
The hunting bird is in your hand, but you don't hunt with it.

The clear glass full of the wine of joy into the dust you throw,
But to the dreadful hangover do you give any thought - no!

In the sleeve of your greedy soul a hundred musk pods you have got,
Yet give them up for the sake of the beloved's hair, this you will not.

In your liver the waves of red blood flow through,
But use it to colour the beloved's face, you won't do.

Your nature's breath isn't musky, for, as the breeze will do,
Passing over the dust of the friend's street you do not do.

I fear from this mead, the rose's sleeve for you may not be,
For from its garden bed a thorn you do not suffer gladly.

Hafiz, go! At the friend's door the service to do,
If it is done by all, yet it is a thing you do not do.

(W-C 495) The radif here is "You make not".
 [1] "...chaugan..." See the glossary in volume one.

Ey del be kooye eshgh gozaari nemikoni

Asbaab ja-m daariyo kaari nemikoni

ای دل به کوی عشق گذاری نمی کنی

اسباب جمع داری و کاری نمی کنی

Chovgaane kaam dar kafo gooee nemizani

Baazi chonin be dasto shekaari nemikoni

چوگان کام در کف و گوئی نمی زنی

بازی چنین به دست و شکاری نمی کنی

Saaghar latifo por meyo miafkani be khaak

Vandishe az balaaye khomaari nemikoni

ساغر لطیف و پر می و می افکنی به خاک

واندیشه از بلای خماری نمی کنی

Dar aastine kaame to sad naafe modraj ast

Vaan raa fadaaye torrye yaari nemikoni

در آستین کام تو صد نافه مدرج است

وان را فدای طرّه یاری نمی کنی

In khoon ke movj mizanad andar jegar to raa

Dar kaare range rooye negaari nemikoni

این خون که موج می زند اندر جگر تو را

در کار رنگ و بوی نگاری نمی کنی

Moshkin az aan nashod dame kholghat ke chon sabaa

Bar khaake kooye doost gozaari nemikoni

مشکین از آن نشد دم خلقت که چون صبا

بر خاک کوی دوست گذاری نمی کنی

Tarsam kazin chaman nabari aastine gol

Kaz golshanash tahammole khaari nemikoni

ترسم کزین چمن نبری آستین گل

کز گلشنش تحمّل خاری نمی کنی

Hafez boro ke bandegiye baargaahe doost

Gar jomle mikonand to baari nemikoni

حافظ برو که بندگی بارگاه دوست

گر جمله می کنند تو باری نمی کنی

Heart, at the time you have become ruined by wine of rose hue,
You have a hundred more dignities than Karun[1], without wealth too.

In that stage where the poor are given governing power,
I anticipate that your rank will be higher than any other.

On the way to where Laila lives, dangers are many,
The first requirement is that Majnun you must be.

Don't ignore the centre point of love shown to you by me,
Or yourself outside of the circle of lovers you will see.

Whilst you slept the caravan has left; ahead only the desert see.
When will you go and who ask the way from? How will it be?

Show the jewel of your essence, if seeking the crown of royalty,
Even if of the lineage of Jamshid and Fereydun you may to be.

Drink wine from the chalice and to the heavens give a drop too,
How long, how long, a liver full of blood will be endured by you.

Don't complain of poverty Hafiz, if this is your poetry,
No one would like to see you sad, whose heart is happy.

(W-C 496) The radif here is "You are".
  [1] "...Karun..." See glossary in volume one.
  [2] "...Layla..." See glossary in volume one for Laila (Layla) and Majnun.

Ey del aan dam ke kharaab az meye gol goon baashi
Bi zaro ganj be sad heshmate ghaaroon baashi

ای دل آن دم که خراب از می گلگون باشی
بی زر و گنج به صد حشمت قارون باشی

Dar maghaami ke sedaarat be faghiraan bakhshand
Chashm daaram ke be jaah az hame afzoon baashi

در مقامی که صدارت به فقیران بخشند
چشم دارم که به جاه از همه افزون باشی

Dar rahe manzele leili ke khatar haast dar aan
Sharte avval ghadam aan ast ke majnoon baashi

در ره منزل لیلی که خطرهاست در آن
شرط اوّل قدم آن است که مجنون باشی

Noghteye eshgh nemoodam be to haan sahv makon
Var na chon bengari az daayere biroon baashi

نقطه عشق نمودم به تو هان سهو مکن
ورنه چون بنگری از دایره بیرون باشی

Kaaravaan rafto to dar khaabo biyaabaan dar pish
Key ravi rah z eke porsi che koni chon baashi

کاروان رفت و تو در خواب و بیابان در پیش
کی روی ره ز که پرسی چه کنی چون باشی

Taaje shaahi talabi govhare zaati benomaay
Var khod az govhare jamshido fereydoon baashi

تاج شاهی طلبی گوهر ذاتی بنمای
ورخود از گوهر جمشید و فریدون باشی

Saaghari nosh kono jor-e bar aflaak feshaan
Chando chand az ghame ayyaam jegar khoon baashi

ساغری نوش کن و جرعه بر افلاک فشان
چند و چند از غم ایّام جگر خون باشی

Hafez az faghr makon naale ke gar sher in ast
Hich khosh del napasandad ke to mahzoon baashi

حافظ از فقر مکن ناله که گر شعر این است
هیچ خوشدل نپسندد که تو محزون باشی

God for the justice of the great Sultan praise be,
Ahmed bin Sheikh Uvais Hasan Ilkhani[1].

Khan son of Khan[2], king descended from most royal ancestry,
If you call him the soul of the world very suitable it would be.

Confidence you inspire whether folk see your fortune or not,
Welcome, you who are worthy and the grace of God have got.

If the moon rises without your say so, split in two it will be,
The fortune of Ahmed[3] and a miracle of one who is all holy.

Both king and beggar lose their heart to your fortune's display,
You are life and beloved, far from you may the evil eye stay.

Put a Turkish curl in your forelock for written in your destiny,
Is the resolve of Chingiz Khan and the generosity of Khagani[4].

We raise the cup to toast you though we are very far, seemingly;
Distance to the resting place is no barrier to the spirit's journey.

From the clay of Fars[5] no rose bud of joy blossomed for me,
Best is the Tigris of Baghdad and wine flavoured fragrantly.

The head of a lover that is not the dust of the beloved's way,
From confusion and distress when will that head find a way.

O Dawn breeze, dust from the beloved's door bring,
So that the eye of the heart Hafiz may be illuminating.

(W-C 497)
[1] *"...Ahmed bin Sheikh Uvais Hasan Ilkhani..." A ruler of Baghdad. See Avery pp.560.*
[2] *"...Khan son of..." King, son of a King.*
[3] *"...Ahmed..." A reference to the above named person but it is also one of the names of the holy prophet Muhammed – one of whose miracles was splitting the moon.*
[4] *"...Chingiz Khan and the generosity of Khagani..." Mongolian rulers.*
[5] *"...Fars..." The part of modern day Iran of which Shiraz is the main city.*

Ahmadollaah alaa ma dalaten soltaani
Ahmade sheykh oveyse hasane ilkaani

احمد الله علی معدله السّلطان
احمد شیخ اویس حسن ایلکانی

Khaane ben khaano shahan shaahe shahan shaah nejaad
Aanke mizibad agar jaane jahaanash khaani

خان بن خان و شهنشاه شهنشاه نژاد
آنکه می زیبد اگر جان جهانش خوانی

Dide naadide be eghbaale to imaan aavard
Marhabaa ey be chonin lotfe khodaa arzaani

دیده نادیده به اقبال تو ایمان آورد
مرحبا ای به چنین لطف خدا ارزانی

Maah agar bi to bar aayad be do nimash bezanand
Dovlate ahmadiyo mojezeye sobhaani

ماه اگر بی تو برآید به دو نیمش بزنند
دولت احمدی و معجزه سبحانی

Jelveye bakhte to del mibarad az shaaho gedaa
Chashme bad door ke ham jaaniyo ham jaanaani

جلوه بخت تو دل می برد از شاه و گدا
چشم بد دور که هم جانی و هم جانانی

Bar shekan kaakole torkaane ke dar taale e tost
Bakhshesho koosheshe khaaghaaniyo changez khaani

برشکن کاکل ترکانه که در طالع تست
بخشش و کوشش خاقانی و چنگزخانی

Gar che doorim be yaade to ghadah migirim
Bo-de manzel nabovad dar safare rovhaani

گرچه دوریم به یاد تو قدح می گیریم
بعد منزل نبود در سفر روحانی

Az gele paarsiyam ghoncheye eyshi nashekoft
Habbazaa dejleye baghdaado meye reyhaani

از گل پارسی ام غنچه عیشی نشکفت
حبّذا دجله بغداد و می ریحانی

Sare aashegh ke na khaake dare mashoogh bovad
Key khalaasash bovad az mehnate sar gardaani

سر عاشق که نه خاک در معشوق بود
کی خلاصش بود از محنت سرگردانی

Ey nasime sahari khaake dare yaar biyaar
Taa konad Hafez azoo dideye del nooraani

ای نسیم سحری خاک در یار بیار
تا کند حافظ ازو دیده دل نورانی

O king of the world's beauties, give redress for our lonely grieving!
The heart is ready to surrender life, surely it is time for your returning.

The freshness of this garden's rose does not last indefinitely,
Help the weak ones whilst you have the opportunity.

Last night, to the wind about your hair I was complaining,
It said, "This is wrong, leave this unwise mode of thinking".

In the chain of that one's hair a hundred dawn breezes dance.
O heart, these are your rivals! Catch the wind? Not a chance!

Separation and longing for you made of me,
One from whose hand patience slips easily.

O Lord, who in the wide world is ready to hear this subtlety,
That, though everywhere, shown to none is that face's beauty.

Saki, without your face the whole rose garden has no colouration,
Walk your tall box-tree form boldly; to give the garden decoration.

For unfulfilled desire, the pain of longing for you is my solution,
Remembering you is the company that I keep in my isolation.

In our destiny's circle we are the compass point of compliance with you,
Kindness is the thought you have and the command is yours to issue.

The way of the profligate is not thought of self or selfishly choosing,
In our religion self appreciation and decision making is not believing.

Due to this sky-blue circle I have a blood filled liver, wine bring,
So that in the blue glass cup this difficulty I can be resolving.

Hafiz, separation's night left; union came, scented sweetly,
O crazy one, wild lover, filled with joy may you always be.

(W-C 498)

[1] "...sky-blue circle...blood filled liver" The sky, or destiny, which has caused his physical nature to be prevalent.

Ey paadshahe khoobaan daad az ghame tanhaaee
Del bi to be jaan aamad vaght ast ke baaz aaee

ای پادشه خوبان داد از غم تنهایی
دل بی تو به جان آمد وقت است که باز آیی

Daaem gole in bostaan shaadaab nemimaanad
Daryaab zaeefaan raa dar vaghte tavaanaaee

دایم گل این بستان شاداب نمی ماند
دریاب ضعیفان را در وقت توانایی

Dishab geleye zolfat baa baad hami kardam
Goftaa ghalati bogzar zin fekrate sovdaaee

دیشب گله زلفت با باد همی کردم
گفتا غلطی بگذر زین فکرت سودایی

Sad baade sabaa aan jaa baa selsele miraghsand
In ast harif ey del taa baad napeymaaee

صد باد صبا آنجا با سلسله می رقصند
این است حریف ای دل تا باد نپیمایی

Moshtaaghiyo mahjoori door az to chonaanam kard
Kaz dast bekhaahad shod paayaabe shakibaaee

مشتاقی و مهجوری دور از تو چنانم کرد
کز دست بخواهد شد پایاب شکیبایی

Yaa rab be ke shaayad goft in nokte ke dar aalam
Rokhsaare be kas nanmood aan shaahede har jaaee

یا رب به که شاید گفت این نکته که در عالم
رخساره به کس ننمود آن شاهد هر جائی

Saaghi chamane gol raa bi rooye to rangi nist
Shemshaad kharaamaan kon taa baagh biyaaraaee

ساقی چمن گل را بی روی تو رنگی نیست
شمشاد خرامان کن تا باغ بیارایی

Ey darde toam darmaan dar bastare naakaami
Vey yaade toam moones dar goosheye tanhaaee

ای درد توأم درمان در بستر ناکامی
وی یاد توأم مونس در گوشه تنهایی

Dar daayereye ghesmat maa noghteye taslimim
Lotf aanche to andishi hokm aanche to far maaee

در دایره قسمت ما نقطه تسلیمیم
لطف آنچه تو اندیشی حکم آنچه تو فرمایی

Fekre khodo raaye khod dar aalame rendi nist
Kofr ast dar in mazhab khod biniyo khod raaee

فکر خود و رای خود در عالم رندی نیست
کفر است در این مذهب خودبینی و خودرایی

Zin daayereye minaa khoonin jegaram mey deh
Taa hal konam in moshkel dar saaghare minaaee

زین دایره مینا خونین جگرم می ده
تا حل کنم این مشکل در ساغر مینایی

Hafez shabe hejraan shod booye khoshe vasl aamad
Shaadit mobarak baad ey aasheghe sheydaaee

حافظ شب هجران شد بوی خوش وصل آمد
شادیت مبارک باد ای عاشق شیدایی

Fragrant incense from the beloved's home, my love increased,
As dust at the friend's door may my precious life be sacrificed.

To hear the friend's message is security and bliss.
To bear my salaams to Su'ad[1]; who will do this?

Come to the 'night of strangers'[2] and the water of my eye see,
Like pure wine in the crystal chalice of Damascus it seems to be.

When the bird of blessings celebrates the owner of the Arak tree[3],
Then from that garden may my dove's cooing not far distant be.

In no time separation from the beloved will be ending,
From the beloved's high abode, I saw the tent tops moving.

Happy the time you come and with a salaam I can say to you,
"Your arrival is blessed, and to a blessed place you came too".

Far from you, I melted into the shape of a crescent moon,
Though I haven't really seen your face like the full moon.

If I am invited to paradise and so break our agreement,
May my spirit not rest easy nor gain any enjoyment[4].

There is a hope that by fortune's favour soon I can see you,
You happy to be commanding, and I to be obeying you.

Hafiz, your verse is like a string of pearls of the highest quality,
With regard to its delicacy it surpasses even the verse of Nizami[5].

(W-C 499)

[1] "...salaams to Su'ad..." This line is in Arabic. Su'ad, according to Avery, is the name of a legendary Arab beloved.

[2] "...the night of strangers..." See glossary under 'Ashura'.

[3] "...Arak tree..." This is a desert tree on which camels feed. The wood of the Arak is used for teeth cleaning and was recommended by the holy Prophet for this purpose. It is also called Siwak.

[4] "...invited to paradise..." Amongst Sufis the goal is not paradise as it is for the orthodox believer – but Allah alone.

[5] "...Nizami..." (d. 1209 AD) He is considered by many to be the greatest epic poet in Persian literature.

Attat ravaa eho randel hemaa va zaada gharaami
Fadaaye khaake dare doost baad jaane geraami

اتت روائح رند الحمی و زاد غرامی
فدای خاک در دوست باد جان گرامی

Payaame doost shanidan sa aadatasto salaamat
Manel moballegho anni elaa soaade salaami

پیام دوست شنیدن سعادت است و سلامت
من المبلغ عنی الی سعاد سلامی

Biyaa be shaame gharibaano aabe dideye man bin
Besaane baadeye saafi dar aab gineye shaamie

بیا به شام غریبان و آب دیده من بین
بسان باده صافی در آبگینه شامی

Ezaa tagharrada an zel araake taaero khayren
Falaa tafarrada an ravzehaa anino hamaami

اذا تغرّد عن ذی الاراک طائر خیر
فلا تفرّد عن روضها انین حمامی

Basi namaand ke rooze feraaghe yaar sar aayad
Ra ayto men hazabaatel hemaa ghebaaba khiyaami

بسی نماند که روز فراق یار سر آید
رایت من هضبات الحمی قباب خیام

Khoshaa dami ke dar aaeeyyo gooyamat be salaamat
Ghademto khayra ghodoomen nazalta khayra maghaami

خوشا دمی که درآئیّ و گویمت به سلامت
قدمت خیر قدوم نزلت خیر مقام

Ba edto menka va ghad serto zaa-eban ka helaalen
Agarche rooye cho maahat nadideam be tamaami

بعدت منک و قد صرت ذائبا کهلال
اگرچه روی چو ماهت ندیده ام به تمامی

Va en doeeto be kholden va serto naagheza ahden
Famaa tatyyaba nafsi va mastataabaa manaami

و ان دعیت بخلد و صرت ناقض عهد
فما تطیّب نفسی و ما استطاب منامی

Omid hast ke zoodat be bakhte nik bebinam
To shaad gashte be farmaandehiyyo man be gholaami

امید هست که زودت به بخت نیک ببینم
تو شاد گشته به فرماندهیّ و من بغلامی

Cho selke dorre khoshaab ast shere naghze to Hafez
Ke gaahe lotf sabagh mibarad ze nazme nezaami

چو سلک درّ خوشاب است شعر نغز تو حافظ
که گاه لطف سبق می برد ز نظم نظامی

O heart, if out from the well of that one's chin you come,
Out of every other place you go only regrets will come.

Be wary for if to the temptation of your nature you succumb,
From Rizvan's[1] paradise garden, like Adam, out you will come.

It's right that from the sky no drop of water to you will come,
If out from the fountain of life, with dry mouth, you come.

Like dawn, my soul yields to the desire to see you come,
Like the shining sun by the way of my door may you come.

How long the breeze-like breath of attention from me should come,
So with joyful cry, out from the rosebud like the rose, you will come.

In the dark of absence my life out from my mouth was ready to come,
It is time now that, splendid as the rising moon, out you should come.

In the dust of your door from my eye a hundred streams come,
So maybe, walking tall like the upright cypress, you will come.

Hafiz, that moon-faced Yusuf[2] will return, don't let worries come:
Then out from the house of sorrow and despair you will come.

(W-C 500) The radif here is "You come out".

[1] "..Rizvan..." The guardian of paradise.

[2] "..Yusuf.." A reference to the prophet Yusuf (Joseph) whose forced separation from his father, Prophet Jacob (Yaqub), caused such sorrow in the older man that he went blind from grief. His sight was restored when he received a shirt prophet Yusuf sent. There are other possible references to the story in the ghazal. For example a reference to the well that prophet Yusuf was dropped into by his brothers (verse 1). He was carnally tempted by Zuleika, his master's wife (verse 2). Other verses read as the longing of prophet Yaqub. 'The dark of absence' perhaps referring to Prophet Yaqub's blindness (verse 6). Maybe there is a suggestion that Prophet Yaqub was spiritually connected to and supporting Prophet Yusuf during his adventures (verse 5). It is possible to read the ghazal as a spiritual conversation between Prophet Yusuf and his father. In the dream prophet Yusuf had at the beginning of his story he saw himself as a sun and his father as the moon (verses 4 and 6). There is also the 'coming out' of prison that plays a key part in the story. See the holy Qur'an; Sura Yusuf.

Ey del gar azaan chaahe zanakhdaan be dar aaee

Har jaa ke ravi zood pashimaan bedar aaee

ای دل گر از آن چاه زنخدان بدر آیی

هر جا که روی زود پشیمان بدر آیی

Hosh daar ke gar vasvaseye nafs koni goosh

Aadam sefat az rovzeye rezvaan bedar aaee

هش دار که گر وسوسه نفس کنی گوش

آدم صفت از روضه رضوان به در آیی

Shaayad ke be aabi falakat dast nagirad

Gar teshne labaz chashmeye heyvaan bedar aaee

شاید که به آبی فلکت دست نگیرد

گر تشنه لبز از چشمه حیوان بدر آیی

Jaan midaham az hasrate didaare to chon sobh

Baashad ke cho khorshide derakhshaan bedar aaee

جان می دهم از حسرت دیدار تو چون صبح

باشد که چو خورشید درخشان بدر آیی

Taa key cho sabaa bar to gomaaram dame hemmat

Kaz ghonche cho gol khorramo khnadaan bedar aaee

تا کی چو صبا بر تو گمارم دم همّت

کز غنچه چو گل خرّم و خندان بدر آیی

Dar tire shabe hejre to jaanam be lab aamad

Vaght ast ke hamchon mahe taabaan be dar aaee

در تیره شب هجر تو جانم به لب آمد

وقت است که همچون مه تابان بدرآیی

Bar khaake darat basteam az dide do sad jooy

Taa boo ke to chon sarve kharaamaan bedar aaee

بر خاک درت بسته ام از دیده دو صد جوی

تا بو که تو چون سرو خرامان بدر آیی

Hafez makon andishe ke aan yoosofe mahrooy

Baaz aayado az kolbeye ahzaan bedar aaee

حافظ مکن اندیشه که آن یوسف مهروی

باز آید و از کلبه احزان بدر آیی

If a letter with the scent of newly black down you would send to me,
Torn up by the turning sphere the page of our existence wouldn't be.

Although the fruit of separation is union indeed,
I wish the Divine Cultivator had not sown that seed.

Forgiveness is the currency of one who currently,
Has a heavenly mansion and a beloved like a Houri.

Turning the Kaaba of the heart[1] into an idol's abode is not just down to me,
A Christian cloister or Jewish synagogue every step of the way one can see.

On the stage of love comfort cannot be expected.
No gold pillow, so with a brick we are contented.

For Iram's garden[2] and its architect's grandiosity don't let go,
A single flagon of wine, one sweet lip, or the edge of a meadow.

O wise heart, grief for this base world, for how long will you be,
It is sad if such a beautiful one should be in love with the ugly.

The stain on the mantle of the Sufi brings about the world's destruction,
Where is a true man of the Way, a man of heart and of pure disposition?

Why has the tip of your long hair been let slip by Hafiz?
What could he do so as not to let it go? For his fate it is.

(W-C 501)
[1] "...Ka'ba of the heart..." Whilst the external building of the Ka'ba in Mecca informs the direction for outer prayer by Muslims, the Sufis speak of the heart as the spiritual Ka'ba.
[2] "...Iram's garden..." Shadad was the architect of the garden of Iram – he built it to imitate paradise.

Aan ghaaliye khat gar sooye maa naame neveshti

Gardoon varaghe hastiye maa dar naneveshti

آن غالیه خط گر سوی ما نامه نوشتی

گردون ورق هستی ما در ننوشتی

Har chand ke hejraan samare vasl bar aarad

Dehghaane jahaan kaaj ke in tokhm nakeshti

هر چند که هجران ثمر وصل برآرد

دهقان جهان کاج که این تخم نکشتی

Aamorzeshe naghd ast kasi raa ke dar injaa

Yaarist cho hooriyyo saraaee cho beheshti

آمرزش نقد است کسی را که در اینجا

یاریست چو حوریّ و سرائی چو بهشتی

Tanhaa na manam kabeye del bot kade karde

Dar har ghadami sovme-ei hasto keneshti

تنها نه منم کعبه دل بتکده کرده

در هر قدمی صومعه ای هست و کنشتی

Dar mastabeye eshgh tanaom natavaan kard

Chon baaleshe zar nist besaazim be kheshti

در مصطبه‌ی عشق تنعّم نتوان کرد

چون بالش زر نیست بسازیم به خشتی

Mafroosh be baaghe eramo nekhvate shaddaad

Yek shishe meyo nooshe labiyyo labe keshti

مفروش به باغ ارم و نخوت شدّاد

یک شیشه می و نوش لبیّ و لب کشتی

Taa key ghame donyaaye dani ey dele daanaa

Heyf ast ze khubi ke shavad aasheghe zeshti

تا کی غم دنیای دنی ای دل دانا

حیف است ز خوبی که شود عاشق زشتی

Aaloodegiye kherghe kharaabiyye jahaan ast

Koo raahrovi ahle deli paak sereshti

آلودگی خرقه خرابیّ جهان است

کو راهروی اهل دلی پاک سرشتی

Az dast cheraa hesht sare zolfe to Hafez

Taghdir chonin ast che kardi ke naheshti

از دست چرا هشت سر زلف تو حافظ

تقدیر چنین است چه کردی که نهشتی

O you who hold it to be lawful to keep lovers separated,
Those fond of you, from your bosom you keep parted.

One thirsting in the desert, with a pure drop, rescue,
On account of the hope for God that this path gives you.

O soul of my life – you stole my heart, and I forgave you,
But I hope you give it better care than I receive from you.

The goblet of ours, others drink from too,
We cannot endure that you allow them to.

O lowly fly, the Simurgh's[1] high palace is not the place for you,
You lose your own dignity and you are a nuisance to us too.

It's your own fault that this door is not available to you,
Who do you complain of? Why make all this hullabaloo?

Promotion is sought from Kings due to one's service,
Without having done any why expect a reward, Hafiz.

(W-C 502) The radif here is "Hold".
   [1] *"...Simurgh..." See glossary in volume one.*
*It is sometimes possible to read ghazals as a dialogue and this would seem to be a case in point. The last three
   verses here being perhaps a response to the earlier verses.*

Ey ke mahjooriye osh shaagh ravaa midaari

Bandegaan raa ze bare khish jodaa midaari

ای که مهجوری عشّاق روا می داری

بندگان را ز بر خویش جدا می داری

Teshneye baadiye raa ham be zolaali daryaab

Be omidi ke darin rah be khodaa midaari

تشنه بادیه را هم به زلالی دریاب

به امیدی که درین ره به خدا می داری

Del roboodiyyo behel kardamat ey jaan likan

Beh azin daar negaahash ke maraa midaari

دل ربودیّ و بحل کردمت ای جان لیکن

به ازین دار نگاهش که مرا می داری

Saaghare maa ke harifaane degar minooshand

Maa tahammol nakonim ar to ravaa midaari

ساغر ما که حریفان دگر می نوشند

ما تحمّل نکنیم ار تو روا می داری

Ey magas hazrate simorgh na jovlaangahe tost

Erze khod mibariyo zahmate maa midaari

ای مگس حضرت سیمرغ نه جولانگه تست

عرض خود می بری و زحمت ما می داری

To be taghsire khod oftaadi azin dar mahroom

Az ke minaaliyo faryaad cheraa midaari

تو به تقصیر خود افتادی ازین در محروم

از که می نالی و فریاد چرا می داری

Hafez az paad shahaan paaye be khedmat talaband

Kaare naakarde che ommide ataa midaari

حافظ از پادشهان پایه به خدمت طلبند

کار ناکرده چه امّید عطا می داری

O you, who only pride in yourself ever take,
Due to your lack of love your excuse we make.

With the crazy lovers don't go hanging about,
Your claim to fame is for wisdom, no doubt.

Love's intoxication hasn't entered into your head,
Go, for you are drunk on the grape's juice instead.

A yellowish face, moaning and groaning,
Are the remedy for the lovers' suffering.

Hafiz, abandon your name and your notoriety,
You are hung over; ask if a cup wine there be.

(W-C 503) The radif here is "You are".

Ey ke daaem be khish maghroori
Gar toraa eshgh nist mazoori

Gerde divaanegaane eshgh magard
Ke be aghle aghile mash hoori

Mastiye eshgh nist dar sare to
Rov ke to maste aabe angoori

Rooye zardasto aahe daraalood
Aasheghaan raa davaaye ranjoori

Bogzar az naamo nange khod Hafez
Saaghare mey talab ke makh moori

گر ترا عشق نیست معذوری
گرد دیوانگان عشق مگرد

که به عقل عقیله مشهوری
مستی عشق نیست در سر تو

رو که تو مست آب انگوری
روی زرد است و آه دردآلود

عاشقان را دوای رنجوری
بگذر از نام و ننگ خود حافظ

ساغر می طلب که مخموری

O you, who in the street of the tavern have a permanent position,
Are the ruler of your own time when a cup is in your possession.

O you who pass days and nights with the beloved's face and hair,
May it be that the time of mornings and evenings are a happy affair.

O breeze of dawn, those burnt with longing on the path are waiting,
For any message you bear from the beloved who has been travelling.

From the smiling lip of the cup the scent of life comes through,
O venerable one, if you have a nose for it, try to detect it too.

If a stranger asks a name[1] from you, is there an issue?
For today in this city a great name is owned by you.

This fresh looking mole of yours is a seed bed for joy to grow,
What a trap though you have planted at the edge of the meadow.

For your life, consistent dawn prayer[2] a guardian troop is,
You who have a slave like the night-vigil keeping Hafiz.

(W-C 504) The radif here is "You have".
   [1] *"..asks a name..." this is not clear. It could refer to the great Name of God.*
   [2] *"..dawn prayer.." Fajr or the prayer made at dawn by Muslims – which Hafiz often mentions.*

Ey ke dar kooye kharaabaat maghaami daari
Jame vaghte khodi ar dast be jaami daari

ای که در کوی خرابات مقامی داری
جم وقت خودی ار دست به جامی داری

Ey ke baa zolfo rokhe yaar gozaari shabo rooz
Forsatat baad ke khosh sobhiyo shaami daari

ای که با زلف و رخ یار گذاری شب و روز
فرصتت باد که خوش صبحی و شامی داری

Ey sabaa sookhtegaan bar sare rah montazerand
Gar azaan yaare safar karde payaami daari

ای صبا سوختگان بر سر ره منتظرند
گر از آن یار سفر کرده پیامی داری

Booye jaan az labe khandaane ghadah mishenavam
Beshno ey khaaje agar zaanke mashaami daari

بوی جان از لب خندان قدح می شنوم
بشنو ای خواجه اگر زانکه مشامی داری

Naami ar mitalabad az to gharibi che shavad
Toee emrooz darin shahr ke naami daari

نامی ار می طلبد از تو غریبی چه شود
توئی امروز درین شهر که نامی داری

Khaale sarsabze to khosh daaneye eyshist vali
Bar kenaare chamanash vah ke che daami daari

خال سرسبز تو خوش دانه عیشیست ولی
بر کنار چمنش وه که چه دامی داری

Bas doaaye saharat haarese jaan khaahad bood
To ke chon Hafeze shab khiz gholami daari

بس دعای سحرت حارس جان خواهد بود
تو که چون حافظ شبخیز غلامی داری

O over the moon a veil of dark musky down you have cast,
A kindness you have done for a shade over the sun you cast.

I wonder what the glowing colour of your face will do to us,
For now it's the spell of a colourless image in water you have cast.

You snatched the ball of beauty from Khollokh's beauties[1], well done!
Try for Kay Khusro's all-seeing cup[2], for by you, out, Afrasyaab is cast[3].

All have ventured to somehow love the candle of your face,
From amongst them it was the moth that into trepidation you cast.

Though I am a drunken sot please don't reject my prayer and plea,
For, in hope of recompense, it was by you into this way I was cast.

The treasure of your love you have hid in the ruins of our heart,
Over the ruined corner the shadow of good fortune you have cast.

Take care, for your glistening face has affected the lions,
Thirsty lipped they are; and heroes into water you have cast.

You bound up the sleep of the sleepless, and then with imagery,
On the troop of sleep's night prowlers, the suspicion you cast.

In the place of revelation you took the face-veil off for just one look,
And in mortification the Houri and Peri behind the veil you cast.

From the world-viewing cup drink wine; for on Jamshid's throne,
From off the face of the desired beloved, the veil you have cast.

With desire for the guileful narcissus, and ruby of wine-worship,
The corner-sitting recluse Hafiz, into wine you have cast.

To capture my heart you threw round my neck the chain of your hair,
Like the noose of the King who is the Lord of necks, you have cast.

O Ruler, with the splendour of Dara![4] You who the crown of the sun,
From the height of power, on to the dust of your doorstep have cast.

Nusratuddin Shah Yayha[5], you, who the country's enemy,
With your fiery flashing blade into the water have cast.

(W-C 505) *The radif here is "You (have) cast".*
  [1] *"..Khollokh's beauties..." According to Avery; an area of Central Asia famed for the beauty of its residents.*
  [2] *"..Kay Khusro's all seeing cup." See glossary in volume one.*
  [3] *"..Afrasyaab..." The ruler of Turan and enemy of the Persians; conquered by Kay Khusro.*
  [4] *"..Dara..." Darius the Great.*
  [5] *"..Nusratuddin Shah Yayha..." He was the nephew of one of Hafiz's patrons; for a while he ruled Shiraz.(see Avery pp 370).*

Ey ke bar maah az khate mokhin neghaab andaakhti
Lotf kardi saayei bar aaftaab andaakhti

ای که بر ماه از خط مشکین نقاب انداختی
لطف کردی سایه ای بر آفتاب انداختی

Taa che khaahad kard baa maa taabo range aarezat
Haaliyaa birang naghshe khod bar aab andaakhti

تا چه خواهد کرد با ما تاب و رنگ عارضت
حالیا بیرنگ نقش خود بر آب انداختی

Gooye khoobi bordi az khoobaane khallokh shaad baash
Jaame key khosrov talab kafraasiyaab andaakhti

گوی خوبی بردی از خوبان خلّخ شاد باش
جام کیخسرو طلب کافراسیاب انداختی

Har kasi baa sham e rokhsaarat be vajhi eshgh baakht
Zaan miyaan parvaane raa dar ezteraab andaakhti

هر کسی با شمع رخسارت به وجهی عشق باخت
زان میان پروانه را در اضطراب انداختی

Taa-ate man gar che az masti kharaabam rad makon
Kandarin shoghlam be ommide savaab andaakhti

طاعت من گرچه از مستی خرابم رد مکن
کاندرین شغلم به امّید ثواب انداختی

Ganje eshghe khod nahaadi dar dele viraane maa
Saayeye dovlat barin konje kharaab andaakhti

گنج عشق خود نهادی در دل ویران ما
سایه دولت برین کنج خراب انداختی

Zinahaar az aabe aan aarez ke shiraan raa azaan
Teshne lab kardiyyo gordaan raa dar aab andaakhti

زینهار از آب آن عارض که شیران را از آن
تشنه لب کردیّ و گردان را در آب انداختی

Khaabe bidaaraan bebasti vaangah az naghshe khiyaal
Tohmati bar shab rovaane kheyle khaab andaakhti

خواب بیداران ببستی وانگه از نقش خیال
تهمتی بر شبروان خیل خواب انداختی

Parde az rokh bar fekandi yek nazar dar jelve gaah
Vaz hayaa hooro pari raa dar hejaab andaakhti

پرده از رخ برفکندی یک نظر در جلوه گاه
وز حیا حور و پری را در حجاب انداختی

Baade noosh az jaame aalam bin ke bar ovrange jam
Shaahede maghsood raa az rokh neghaab andaakhti

باده نوش از جام عالم بین که بر اورنگ جم
شاهد مقصود را از رخ نقاب انداختی

Az faribe nargese makhmooro la-le may parast
Hafeze khalvat neshin raa dar sharaab andaakhti

از فریب نرگس مخمور و لعل می پرست
حافظ خلوت نشین را در شراب انداختی

Vaz baraaye seyde del dar gardanam zanjire zolf
Chon kamande khosrove maalek reghaab andaakhti

وز برای صید دل در گردنم زنجیر زلف
چون کمند خسرو مالک رقاب انداختی

Daavare daaraa shokooh ey aanke taaje aaftaab
Az sare ta-zim bar khaake jenaab anadaakhti

داور داراشکوه ای آنکه تاج آفتاب
از سر تعظیم بر خاک جناب انداختی

Nosrateddin shaah yahyaa aanke khasme molk raa
Az dame shamshire chon aatash dar aab andaakhti

نصرت الدّین شاه یحیی آنکه خصم ملک را
از دم شمشیر چون آتش در آب انداختی

O you! Your face shines with the splendours of sovereignty,
In your thought you conceal a hundred wisdoms of divinity.

God be pleased! In the religion and the country, from your pen,
A thousand fonts of the water of life one drop of ink made open.

On the devil will not shine the splendours of the Great Name,[1]
The country and seal ring are yours. What you want, just name.

On the sovereignty of Solomon, if doubt someone is casting
Even fish and birds mock at that one's wit and learning.

Though the hawk sometimes dons the crown of royalty,
The birds of Kaf[2] know the real meaning of sovereignty.

The sword whose lustre is from heaven's spring of bounty,
Can conquer the whole world without the help of an army.

For the close friend and distant stranger, your pen writes well,
Life protecting charms for one; for the other a life ending spell.

O you, in your nature pride is founded on the sense of honour,
And, o you whose fortune is secure from ruination's danger.

If a beam of light flashes from your sword on mine and quarry,
Into the yellow of withered grass turns the red-faced ruby.

O King, it is a lifetime that, of wine, this cup of mine is empty,
This slave now presses his claim, and the guard gives testimony.

On night-waker's weakness your heart I know has mercy,
If, about my state, from the morning breeze you make inquiry.

O Saki, from the fountain of the tavern bring us a little water,
So we may cleanse our Sufi robes of the pride of the Khanqah[3].

When the lightning of sin struck Adam in his purity,
How can we make any claim to be free of iniquity?

Hafiz, since the King mentions your name occasionally,
Don't complain of fortune; return and say you're sorry.

(W-C 506)
   [1] "...Great Name..." Isme-Azam, the hidden great name of God.
   [2] "...Kaf..." (Qaf) See glossary in volume one.
   [3] "...Khanqah..." A place in which Sufis gather for collective practices such as zikr.
According to W-C this ghazal is addressed to Nusratuddin Shah Yahya (see above).

Ey dar rokhe to peydaa anvaare paad shaahi
Dar fekrate to penhaan sad hekmate elaahi

ای در رخ تو پیدا انوار پادشاهی
در فکرت تو پنهان صد حکمت الهی

Kelke to baarekallah bar molko din goshaade
Sad cheshme aabe heyvaan az ghatrei siyaahi

کلک تو بارک الله بر ملک و دین گشاده
صد چشمه آب حیوان از قطره ای سیاهی

Bar ahreman nataabad anvaare esme azam
Molke aane tosto khaatam famamaay har che khaahi

بر اهرمن نتابد انوار اسم اعظم
ملک آن تست و خاتم فرمای هر چه خواهی

Dar heshmate soleymaan har kas ke shak namaayad
Bar aghlo daaneshe ou khandand morgho maahi

در حشمت سلیمان هر کس که شک نماید
بر عقل و دانش او خندند مرغ و ماهی

Baaz arche gaah gaahi bar sar nahad kolaahi
Morghaane ghaaf daanand aaeene paadshaahi

باز ار چه گاهگاهی بر سر نهد کلاهی
مرغان قاف دانند آئین پادشاهی

Tighi ke aasemaanash az feyze khod dahad aab
Tanhaa jahaan begirad bi mennate sepaahi

تیغی که آسمانش از فیض خود دهد آب
تنها جهان بگیرد بی منّت سپاهی

Kelke to khosh nevisad dar sha-ne yaaro aghyaar
Ta-vize jaan fazaaee afsoone omr kaahi

کلک تو خوش نویسد در شأن یار و اغیار
تعویذ جان فزائی افسون عمر کاهی

Ey onsore to makhloogh az kebriyaaye ezzat
Vey dovlate to imen az sadmeye tabaahi

ای عنصر تو مخلوق از کبریای عزّت
وی دولت تو ایمن از صدمه تباهی

Gar partovi ze tighat bar kaano madan oftad
Yaaghoote sorkhroo raa bakhshand range kaahi

گر پرتوی ز تیغت بر کان و معدن افتد
یاقوت سرخ رو را بخشند رنگ کاهی

Omrist paad shaahaa kaz mey tohist jaamam
Inak ze bande davi vaz mohtaseb govaahi

عمری ست پادشاها کز می تهیست جامم
اینک ز بنده دعوی وز محتسب گواهی

Daanam delat bebakhshad bar ajze shab neshinaan
Gar haale man beporsi az baade sobh gaahi

دانم دلت ببخشد بر عجز شب نشینان
گر حال من بپرسی از باد صبحگاهی

Saaghi biyaar aabi az cheshmeye kharaabaat
Taa kherghehaa beshooeem az ojbe khaanghaahi

ساقی بیار آبی از چشمه خرابات
تا خرقه ها بشوییم از عجب خانقاهی

Jaaee ke barghe esyaan bar aadame safi zad
Maa raa chegoone zibad daviyye bi gonaahi

جائی که برق عصیان بر آدم صفی زد
ما را چگونه زیبد دعوی بیگناهی

Hafez cho paad shaahat gah gaah mibarad naam
Ranjesh ze bakht man maa baazaa be ozr khaahi

حافظ چو پادشاهت گه گاه می برد نام
رنجش ز بخت منما بازآ به عذر خواهی

O you! From your street, the tale of paradise is just one story;
From your face the tale of the Houri's beauty is just one story.

Beside Your ruby lip Jesus' breaths[1] are not a big matter,
Of your mouth's sweetness Khizr's water is but an indicator.

Every part of my fragmented heart has a history of grief,
Every line on your qualities is a verse about mercy's relief.

The rose, perfuming the assembly of kindred souls, how could it,
If with the blessing of your scent you had not endowed it?

Longing for the dust of beloved's door has burnt us,
Dawn breeze, remember, no aid did you send to us.

Heart, you have spent life and knowledge vanities pursuing,
A hundred revenue streams you had yet you achieved nothing.

The smell of my roasted heart spanned the world's far horizon,
May this fire burning within me have a similar penetration.

If it is that your image appears in this conflagration,
Come Saki, I complain not if hell is the destination.

In this pain do you know what Hafiz is really seeking?
An inviting look from you, and a boon from the king.

(W-C 507)

[1] "...The breaths of Jesus..." The breath of Lord Jesus was the means of his many miracles in restoring the sick to health. It is associated with the way he himself was given life by Angel Gabriel.

Ey ghesseye behesht ze kooyat hekaayati

Sharhe jamaale hoor ze rooyat revaayati

ای قصّه بهشت ز کویت حکایتی

شرح جمال حور ز رویت روایتی

Anfaase isi az labe la-lat letife ee

Vaabe khezer ze nooshe dahaanat kenaayati

انفاس عیسی از لب لعلت لطیفه ای

واب خضر ز نوش دهانت کنایتی

Har paare az dele man vaz ghosse ghessei

Har satri az khesaale to vaz rahmat aayati

هر پاره از دل من و از غصّه قصّه ای

هر سطری از خصال تو وز رحمت آیتی

Key atr saaye majlese roohaaniyaan shodi

Gol raa agar na booye to kardi re aayati

کی عطرسای مجلس روحانیان شدی

گل را اگر نه بوی تو کردی رعایتی

Dar aarezooye khaake dare yaar sookhtim

Yaad aavar ey sabaa ke nakardi hemaayati

در آرزوی خاک در یار سوختیم

یاد آور ای صبا که نکردی حمایتی

Ey del be harze daanesho omrat ze dast raft

Sad maaye daashtiyyo nakardi kefaayati

ای دل به هرزه دانش و عمرت ز دست رفت

صد مایه داشتیّ و نکردی کفایتی

Booye dele kabaabe man aafaagh raa gereft

In aatashe daroon bekonad ham seraayati

بوی دل کباب من آفاق را گرفت

این آتش درون بکند هم سرایتی

Dar aatash ar khiyaale rokhash dast midahad

Saaghi biyaa ke nist ze doozakh shekaayati

در آتش از خیال رخش دست می دهد

ساقی بیاکه نیست ز دوزخ شکایتی

Daani moraade Hafez azin dardo ghosse chist

Az to kereshmeiyyo ze khosro enaayati

دانی مراد حافظ ازین درد و غصّه چیست

از تو کرشمه ای و ز خسرو عنایتی

That I put this Sufi garb in pawn for wine, for me is best,
And that this nonsense book I drown in wine, for me is best.

Since, as far as I can see, a ruin I made of my life,
To collapse into the corner of the tavern, for me is best.

Since the dervish does not consider expediency to be good,
A heart filled with fire and an eye with water, for me is best.

Of the pious abstainer's heart state I won't tell anyone,
To tell this tale only to harp and rebab, this for me is best.

In as much as this sphere's order is headless and legless,
A head wanting the Saki, and wine in hand, for me is best.

Yes, from a beloved like you I won't withdraw my heart,
If the curls in your hair are a torment, that for me is best.

Hafiz, depart from the tavern, since you have grown old,
The desire's of the Rend are for youth, that is when it's best.

(W-C 508) The radif here is "Best". We have made use of the radif in this version.

In kherghe ke man daaram dar rahne sharaan ovlaa
Vin daftare bi ma-ni gharghe meye naab ovlaa

این خرقه که من دارم در رهن شراب اولی
وین دفتر بی معنی غرق می ناب اولی

Chon omr tabah kardam chandaan ke negah kardam
Dar konje kharaabaati oftaade kharaab ovlaa

چون عمر تبه کردم چندان که نگه کردم
در کنج خراباتی افتاده خراب اولی

Chon maslahat andishi door ast ze darvishi
Ham sine por az aatash ham dide por aab ovlaa

چون مصلحت اندیشی دور است ز درویشی
هم سینه پر از آتش هم دیده پر آب اولی

Man haale dele zaahed baa khalgh nakhaaham goft
In ghesse agar gooyam baa chango robaab ovlaa

من حال دل زاهد با خلق نخواهم گفت
کاین قصّه اگر گویم با چنگ و رباب اولی

Taa bi saro paa baashad ovzaae falak zin dast
Dar sar havase saaghi dar dast sharaab ovlaa

تا بی سر و پا باشد اوضاع فلک زین دست
در سر هوس ساقی در دست شراب اولی

Az hamcho to deldaari del bar nakanam aari
Cho taab kesham baari zaan zolfe betaab ovlaa

از همچو تو دلداری دل برنکنم آری
چون تاب کشم باری زان زلف بتاب اولی

Chon pir shodi Hafez az meykade biroon aay
Rendiyyo havas naaki dar ahde shabaab ovlaa

چون پیر شدی حافظ از میکده بیرون آی
رندیّ و هوسناکی در عهد شباب اولی

O you who show no mercy when killing us is the issue,
You burn up capital and interest, not caring what you do.

In the possession of pain sufferers is something poisonous,
Don't even think of plotting against this tribe, it's dangerous.

When a glance from the corner of your eye can end our pain,
It's just not justice that from giving this cure you should refrain

Since in the hope for you our eye became a sea,
Why not come to the shore in order to sightsee.

The tales they tell of hurts that your merciful nature is said to do,
Are the words of prejudiced people. Such things are not from you.

O pious man, if our beloved were to be revealed to you,
You'll ask of God nothing but the beloved and wine too.

Hafiz, the beloved's eyebrow is the arch for prostrating in prayer,
Your supplication won't carry sincerity unless you make it there.

(W-C 509) The radif here is "You make (or show) not".

Ey ke dar koshtane maa hich modaaraa nakoni
Soodo sarmaaye besooziyyo mohaabaa nakoni

Dard mandaane balaa zahre halaahel daarand
Ghasde in ghovm khatar baashad haan taa nakoni

Ranje maa raa ke tavaan bord be yek goosheye chashm
Sharte ensaaf nabaashad ke modaavaa nakoni

Dideye maa cho be ommide to daryaast cheraa
Be tafarroj gozari bar labe daryaa nakoni

Naghle har jovr ke az kholghe karimat kardand
Ghovle saaheb ghara zaanast to anhaa nakoni

Bar to gar jelve konad shaahede maa ey zaahed
Az khodaa joz meyo mashoogh tamannaa nakoni

Hafezaa sajde be abrooye cho mehraabash bar
Ke doaaee ze sare sedgh jozaanjaa nakoni

ای که در کشتن ما هیچ مدارا نکنی
سود و سرمایه بسوزیّ و محابا نکنی

دردمندان بلا زهر هلاهل دارند
قصد این قوم خطر باشد هان تا نکنی

رنج ما را که توان برد به یک گوشه چشم
شرط انصاف نباشد که مداوا نکنی

دیده ما چو به امّید تو دریاست چرا
به تفرّج گذری بر لب دریا نکنی

نقل هر جور که از خلق کریمت کردند
قول صاحب غرضان است تو آنها نکنی

بر تو گر جلوه کند شاهد ما ای زاهد
از خدا جز می و معشوق تمنّا نکنی

حافظا سجده به ابروی چو محرابش بر
که دعائی ز سر صدق جز آنجا نکنی

O you without news, try hard, so that possessor of news you be,
If you are not traveller on the way, how then a guide can you be?

In the school of truths, before a possessor of love's courtesy,
My dear son, try hard so that one day a father you may be.

Like true men of the Way, the copper of self existence spurn,
And so possess the chemistry of love, and into gold turn[1].

Sleeping and eating took you far from the status that you merit,
When food and sleep you deny, you will take possession of it.

If in your heart and life the light of love of Truth were to fall, then,
By God, you would possess more brightness than the sun in heaven.

Though you immerse yourself a moment in the sea of Divinity, yet,
From all the seven seas not a single hair of yours will become wet.

From toe to top of the head possessed by the light of God you will be,
If, you become headless and footless in the Way of God's Majesty.

If in the sanctuary of sight the Face of God you may see,
Then without doubt the possessor of vision you will be.

If the foundation of your existence is overturned completely,
About being turned upright again, do not let your heart worry.

Hafiz, if desire for union in your head there be,
Dust of the door of virtue possessors you must be.

(W-C 510) The radif here is "You may (or shall) be".
  [1] *"...and into gold..." This is reference to alchemy, often used as a metaphor for spiritual transformation. One understanding of this ghazal is that it is advice to a youth.*

Ey bi khabar bekoosh ke saaheb khabar shavi
Taa raahrov nabaashi key raahbar shavi

ای بیخبر بکوش که صاحب خبر شوی
تا راهرو نباشی کی راهبر شوی

Dar maktabe haghaayegh pishe adibe eshgh
Haan ey pesar bekoosh ke roozi pedar shavi

در مکتب حقایق پیش ادیب عشق
هان ای پسر بکوش که روزی پدر شوی

Dast az mese vojood cho mardaane rah beshooy
Taa kimiyaaye eshgh biyaabiyyo zar shavi

دست از مس وجود چو مردان ره بشوی
تا کیمیای عشق بیابیّ و زر شوی

Khaabo khorat ze martabeye khish door kard
Aangar rasi be khish ke bi khaabo khor shavi

خواب و خورت ز مرتبه خویش دور کرد
آنگه رسی به خویش که بی خواب و خور شوی

Gar noore eshghe hagh be delo jaanat oof tad
Bellah kaz aaftaabe falak khoob tar shavi

گر نور عشق حق به دل و جانت اوفتد
بالله کز آفتاب فلک خوبتر شوی

Yek dam gharighe bahre khodaa sho gamaan mabar
Kaz aabe haft bahr be yek mooy tar shavi

یک دم غریق بحرخدا شو گمان مبر
کز آب هفت بحربه یک موی تر شوی

Az paay taa sarat hame noore khodaa shavad
Dar raahe zol jalaal cho bi paavo sar shavi

از پای تا سرت همه نور خدا شود
در راه ذوالجلال چو بی پا و سر شوی

Vajhe khodaa agar shavadat manzare nazar
Zin pas shaki namaand ke saaheb nazar shavi

وجه خدا اگر شودت منظر نظر
زین پس شکی نماند که صاحب نظر شوی

Bonyaade hastiye to cho ziro zebar shavad
Dar del madaar hich ke ziro zebar shavi

بنیاد هستی تو چو زیر و زبر شود
در دل مدار هیچ که دیگر زبر شوی

Gar dar sarat havaaye vesaal ast Hafeza
Baayad ke khaake dargahe ahle honar shavi

گر در سرت هوای وصال است حافظا
باید که خاک درگه اهل هنر شوی

Don't speak of love's mysteries or intoxication to one who opposes,
So that unenlightened, in the pain of self-worship, to death he goes.

In spite of being weak and poorly be happy as the breeze,
On this path, better than being at ease, is to have disease.

Whilst you see learning and reason as best, enlightened you won't be;
But one thing I will tell you, don't regard yourself in order to be free.

When at the beloved's door, pay no heed to heaven at all,
Or to the dust of lowness from that high place you may fall[1].

Be a lover, for, if you are not, the world's work will come to a conclusion,
But you will not have read what is the workshop of existence's intention.

Immaturity is unbelief in the teachings of the Sufi Way,
To gain joy on this road agility and quickness are the way.

How can one try to hide away and in a corner to have ease,
Whilst your narcissus eye tells to us its drunken mysteries.

On that day I saw how it is that fortune treated us so badly,
When you scorned for a while to keep us company.

Though the thorn shortens life, excuses for it the rose tries to make.
By its intoxicating pleasure wine's bitterness is made easy to take.

The Sufi drinks from a cup, but Hafiz of the wine keg be minded.
You with short sleeves[2], how far your greedy grasp is extended.

(W-C 511)
   [1] In other words, this verse is saying, even heaven is a low place compared to the dust of the Beloved's door.
   [2] "...with short sleeves..." A mean person.
(W-C 512) See glossary.

Baa moddaee magooeed asraare eshgho masti
Taa bi khabar bemirad dar darde khod parasti

با مدّعی مگوئید اسرار عشق و مستی
تا بی خبر بمیرد دردرد خود پرستی

Baa za-fo naatavaani hamchon nasim khosh baash
Bimaari andarin rah behtar ze tan dorosti

با ضعف و ناتوانی همچون نسیم خوش باش
بیماری اندرین ره خوشتر ز تندرستی

Taa fazlo aghl bini bi marefat neshini
Yek nokteat begooyam khod raa mabin ke rasti

تا فضل و عقل بینی بی معرفت نشینی
یک نکته ات بگویم خود را مبین که رستی

Dar aastaane jaanaan az aasemaan mayandish
Kaz ovje sar bolandi ofti be khaake pasti

در آستان جانان از آسمان میندیش
کز اوج سربلندی افتی به خاک پستی

Aashegh sho ar na roozi kaare jahaan sar aayad
Naa khaande naghshe maghsood az kaargaahe hasti

عاشق شو ارنه روزی کار جهان سر آید
ناخوانده نقش مقصود از کارگاه هستی

Dar mazhabe tarighat khaami neshaane kofr ast
Aari tarighe dovlat chaalaaki asto chosti

در مذهب طریقت خامی نشان کفر است
آری طریق دولت چالاکی است و چستی

Dar goosheye salaamat mastoor chon tavaan bood
Taa nargese to baa maa gooyad romooze masti

در گوشه سلامت مستور چون توان بود
تا نرگس تو با ما گوید رموز مستی

Aan rooz dide boodam aan fetnehaa ke bar khaast
Kaz sarkeshi zamaani baa maa nemi neshasti

آن روز دیده بودم آن فتنه ها که برخاست
کز سرکشی زمانی با ما نمی نشستی

Khaar ar che jaan bekaahad gol ozre aan bekhaahad
Sahl ast talkhiye mey dar jambe zovghe masti

خار از چه جان بکاهدگل عذر آن بخواهد
سهل است تلخی می در جنب ذوق مستی

Soofi piyaale peymaa Hafez gharaabe parhiz
Ey kootah aastinaan taa key deraaz dasti

صوفی پیاله پیما حافظ قرابه پرهیز
ای کوته آستینان تا کی دراز دستی

Hear this subtlety from me, so that free from grief you may be,
Seek bounty not meant for you and blood-drinking you will be.

Tomorrow you will become the potter's clay,
At least be filling the jug with wine today.

If you are one of those who in paradise want to be,
A number of those who are Pari-like[1] take for company.

You cannot presume to occupy the throne of the mighty,
Unless all of the concomitant causes you have made ready.

O king of the sweet lipped ones, rewards are waiting,
If towards fallen-hearted Farhad[2] a glance you are giving.

How can your heart be ready for the image of bounty,
Unless you cleanse it of its multitudinous imagery.

If you gave your work into the hand of the Generous[3], Hafiz,
How much you would enjoy the fortune that God-given is.

O dawn breeze, do Khwaja Jalaluddin's[4] bidding,
And the world with Jasmine and Lily be filling.

(W-C 513)

[1] "...Pari-like..." Spiritually beautiful.
[2] "...Farhad..." See glossary in volume one.
[3] "...the Generous..." One of God's Beautiful Names.
[4] "...Khwaja Jalaluddin..." According to Avery this refers to the Vizier of one of Hafiz's patrons, Shah Shuja.

Beshno in nokte ke khod raa ze gham aazaade koni
Khoon khori gar talabe rooziye nan haade koni

بشنو این نکته که خود را ز غم آزاده کنی
خون خوری گر طلب روزی ننهاده کنی

Aakherol amr gele kooze garaan khaahi shod
Haliyaa fekre saboo kon ke por az baade koni

آخرالامر گل کوزه گران خواهی شد
حالیا فکر سبو کن که پر از باده کنی

Gar az aan aadamiyaani ke beheshtat havas ast
Eysh ba aadamei chand pari zaade koni

گر از آن آدمیانی که بهشتت هوس است
عیش با آدمی چند پریزاده کنی

Tekye bar jaaye bozorgaan natavaan zad be gazaaf
Magar asbaabe bozorgi hame aamaade koni

تکیه بر جای بزرگان نتوان زد به گزاف
مگر اسباب بزرگی همه آماده کنی

Ajrhaa baashadat ey khosrove shirin dahanaan
Gar negaahi sooye farhaade del oftaade koni

اجرها باشدت ای خسرو شیرین دهنان
گر نگاهی سوی فرهاد دل افتاده کنی

Khaaterat key raghame feyz pazirad heyhaat
Magar az naghshe paraakande varagh saade koni

خاطرت کی رقم فیض پذیرد هیهات
مگر از نقش پراکنده ورق ساده کنی

Kaare khod gar be karam baaz gozaari Hafez
Ey basaa eysh ke baa bakhte khodaa daade koni

کار خود گر به کرم باز گذاری حافظ
ای بسا عیش که با بخت خداداده کنی

Ey sabaa bandegiye khaaje jaleddin kon
Ke jahaan por samano soosane aazaade koni

ای صبا بندگی خواجه جلال الدّین کن
که جهان پر سمن و سوسن آزاده کنی

If to the voice of the bulbul and turtle-dove you are not drinking,
What cure can there be? The treatment of last resort is burning.

Stock up with the colour and scent of the spring season,
For those bandits, the winter months, are coming on.

Since the rose took off the veil and the bird sings "Hoo hoo" gladly[1],
Don't put down the cup! Why is it "Hai, Hai" that you say so sadly.

Hoarding up what one has inherited, amounts to apostasy,
Musician and Saki say this, and drum and flute thus decree.

When in your hand is the water of life from thirst do not die,
Everything that is living gets its life from water. Do not die[2].

Whatever time gives it takes away again, ultimately,
Don't expect anything at all from one so miserly.

On the gate of a garden of the mansion of paradise inscribed is;
"For whoever has brought worldly attraction, bad news there is".

Generosity is no more! I cut short the speech; Wine, where is it?
For the soul's joy and to celebrate the life of Hatim Tai[3], give it.

No miser has the scent of God's generosity. Come on Hafiz,
Take the cup of wine, be liberal, for you my guarantee there is.

(W-C 514)
[1] "..Hoo.....Hai..." Hoo here represents the sound of a bird but also the term used for the ipseity of Allah. His 'isness'. According to W-C "Hai" is the sound for "alas" in Farsi.
[2] This line is in Arabic and is said to found inscribed often on drinking fountains and wells.
[3] "..."Hatim Tai..." A fabulously wealthy and very generous man.
(W-C 515) See appendix.

Be sovte bolbolo ghomri agar nanooshi mey
Elaaj key konamat aakherod davaa al key

به صوت بلبل و قمری اگر ننوشی می
علاج کی کنمت آخرالّدوا الکیّ

Zakhirei benehaz rango booye fasle bahaar
Ke miresand ze pey rahzanaane bahmano dey

ذخیره ای بنه از رنگ و بوی فصل بهار
که می رسند ز پی رهزنان بهمن و دی

Cho gol neghaab barafkando morgh zad hoo hoo
Maneh ze dast piyaale che mikoni hey hey

چو گل نقاب برافکند و مرغ زد هوهو
منه ز دست پیاله چه می کنی هی هی

Khazine daariye miraas khaaregaagan kofr ast
Be ghovle motrebo saghi be fatviye dafo ney

خزینه داری میراث خوارگان کفر است
به قول مطرب و ساقی به فتوی دف و نی

Cho hast aabe hayaatat be dast teshne mamir
Falaa tamot va menal maae kollo shayen hay

چو هست آب حیاتت به دست تشنه ممیر
فلا تمت و من الماء کل شیء حی

Zamaane hich nabakhshad ke baaz nastaanad
Majoo ze sefle morovvat ke shayohoo laa shey

زمانه هیچ نبخشد که باز نستاند
مجو ز سفله مروّت که شیئه لا شی

Neveshteand bar eyvaane jannatol mavaa
Ke har ke eshveye donyaa kharid vaay be vey

نوشته اند بر ایوان جنّه المأوی
که هر که عشوه دنیا خرید وای به وی

Sakhaa namaand sokhan tey konam sharaab kojaast
Bede be shaadiye rooho ravaane haatame tey

سخا نماند سخن طی کنم شراب کجاست
بده به شادی روح و روان حاتم طی

Bakhil booye khodaa nashnavad biyaa Hafez
Piyaale giro karam varz vazzamaano alay

بخیل بوی خدا نشنود بیا حافظ
پیاله گیر و کرم ورز و الضّمان علی

Your beauty's art is as perfect as my love is,
Be happy about it, for this beauty unending is.

Reason cannot begin to think that in the imagination,
Anything could ever come that can bear comparison.

Our entire life would be fulfilled if, with you, Union we gain,
Even if for only a single day this provision we obtain.

When I am with you, a year but a single day seems to be,
When I am without you, an instant seems a year to me.

Beloved how can your face appear in sleep to me?
When a dream image of you is all I can ever see.

For loving your face, so fair, show my heart some mercy;
Thin as the crescent moon my feeble body has grown to be.

Complain not, if union with the beloved you want Hafiz,
You should endure separation more patiently than this.

(W-C 516) Separation.

Begreft kaare hosnat chon eshghe man kamaali
Khosh baash zaanke nabvad in hosn raa zavaali

بگرفت کار حسنت چون عشق من کمالی
خوش باش زانکه نبود این حسن را زوالی

Dar vahm mi nagonjad kandar tasavvore aghl
Aayad be hich ma-ni zin khoobtar mesaali

در وهم می نگنجد کاندر تصوّرعقل
آید به هیچ معنی زین خوبتر مثالی

Shod hazze omr haasel gar zaanke baa to ma raa
Hargez be omre roozi roozi shavad vesaali

شد حظّ عمر حاصل گر زانکه با تو ما را
هرگز به عمر روزی روزی شود وصالی

Aan dam ke baa to baasham yek saal hast roozi
Vaan dam ke bi to baasham yek lahze hast saali

آن دم که با تو باشم یک سال هست روزی
وان دم که بی تو باشم یک لحظه هست سالی

Chon man khiyaale rooyat jaanaa be khaab binam
Kaz khaab mi nabinad chashmam bejoz khiyaali

چون من خیال رویت جانا به خواب بینم
کز خواب می نبیند چشمم بجز خیالی

Rahm aar bar dele man kaz mehre rooye khoobat
Shod shakhse naatavaanam baarik chon helaali

رحم آر بر دل من کز مهر روی خوبت
شد شخص ناتوانم باریک چون هلالی

Hafez makon shekaayat gar vasle doost khaahi
Zin bishtar bebaayad bar hejrat ehtemaali

حافظ مکن شکایت گر وصل دوست خواهی
زین بیشتر بباید بر هجرت احتمالی

The bulbul, calling from the branch of the cypress tree, in Pahlavi[1],
Last night was reciting lessons, describing the stages of spirituality[2].

It was saying, "Come, for the fire Moses saw, the rose shows clearly,
And so from the bush hear described the subtle nature of divine unity".[2]

The garden birds make up humorous sayings with rhyming,
So the respected elder has Pahlavi Ghazals whilst wine drinking.

Happy days, sleeping on the mat of poverty, in safety,
Kings on thrones do not have the benefit of this luxury.

From this world Jamshid left with nothing but that cup's story,
Beware! Don't let your heart be enmeshed in the world's glory.

Hear a story that is topsy-turvy and really surprising,
With the breaths of Jesus, us the beloved was killing.

The houses of the folk are destroyed when you look so archly,
May you not get hung-over, for wine makes you walk so drunkenly.

The old farmer spoke to his son, and sage was his, saying,
"O light of my eye, you will reap whatever you are sowing".

Could it be the Saki gave some extra to Hafiz?
For in disarray the turban of the Maulevi is.

(W-C 517)

[1] *"..Pahlavi..." An ancient Persian Language.*

[2] *The second part of the verse is believed by Avery and W-C to indicate the Masnevi of Maulana Jalaluddin Rumi.*

[3] *"...the fire that Moses saw..." A reference to Moses and the burning bush, which can be found in the holy Bible and the holy Qur'an. In this case the Masnevi could be the 'bush' in the second verse; the garden bird's rhymed saying could likewise refer to the Masnevi which is in rhymed couplets. Maulana Rumi also draws moral lessons from stories and this may be what is evoked in the penultimate line. The turbans associated with the Order Maulana (Mevlana) founded in Konya, Turkey have folded cloth wrapped round the base of a tall round felt hat.*

Bolbol ze shaakhe sarv be golbaange pahlavi
Mikhaand doosh darse maghaamaate manavi

بلبل ز شاخ سرو به گلبانگ پهلوی
می خواند دوش درس مقامات معنوی

Yani biyaa ke aatashe moosaa nemood gol
Taa az derakht nokteye tovheed beshnavi

یعنی بیا که آتش موسی نمود گل
تا از درخت نکته توحید بشنوی

Morghaane baagh ghaafiye sanjando bazle gooy
Taa khaaje mey khorad be ghazal haaye pahlavi

مرغان باغ قافیه سنجند و بذله گوی
تا خواجه می خورد به غزلهای پهلوی

Khosh vaghte booriyaaye gedaaeeyyo khaabe amn

خوش وقت بوریای گدائی و خواب امن
کاین عیش نیست روزی اورنگ خسروی

Kin eysh nist rooziye ovrange khosravi
Jamshid joz hekaayate jaam az jahaan nabord
Zen haar del maband dar asbaabe donyavi

جمشید جز حکایت جام از جهان نبرد
زنهار دل مبند در اسباب دنیوی

In ghesseye ajab sheno az bakhte vaajgoon
Maaraa bekosht yaar be anfaase isavi

این قصّه عجب شنو از بخت واژگون
ما را بکشت یار به انفاس عیسوی

Chashmat be eshve khaaneye mardom kharaab kard
Makhmooriyat mabaad ke khosh mast miravi

چشمت به عشوه خانه مردم خراب کرد
مخموریت مباد که خوش مست می روی

Dehghaane saal khorde che khosh goft baa pesar
Key noore chashme man bejoz az keshte nadravi

دهقان سالخورده چه خوش گفت با پسر
کای نور چشم من بجز از کشته ندروی

Saaghi magar vazifeye Hafez ziyaade daad
Kaashofte gasht torreye dastaare movlavi

ساقی مگر وظیفه حافظ زیاده داد
کاشفته گشت طرّه دستار مولوی

Come, O idol, and to us do not show enmity,
Since the days of old we have kept company.

Listen to what I say for its value is much more,
Than the jewel that in the treasure chest you store.

Come and heed the poor hung-over ones that cry,
If, for God's sake, last night's wine you can supply.

But how to the Rends[1] can you ever show your face,
When for the sun and moon you have the mirror case.

Sheikh, about the Rends do not speak ill, be wary,
Lest with God's love you should have enmity!

Afraid of the fiery nature of my sigh, are you not?
You know the robe you wear is woollen[2], do you not?

Your verse is more beautiful than any I have seen, Hafiz,
This I say on the holy Qur'an that in your heart there is.

(W-C 518) The radif here is "You have".
   [1] "...Rends..." Profligates. See glossary in volume one.
   [2] "...the robe you wear is woollen..." He implies here it can be easily burnt by a sigh.

Botaa baa maa mavarz in kine daari

Ke hagh ghe sohbate dirine daari

بتا با ما مورز این کینه داری

که حقّ صحبت دیرینه داری

Nasihat goosh kon kin dor basi beh

Az aan govhar ke dar ganjine daari

نصیحت گوش کن کاین در بسی به

از آن گوهر که در گنجینه داری

Be faryaade khomaare moflesaan ras

Khodaa raa gar meye dooshine daari

به فریاد خمار مفلسان رس

خدا را گر می دوشینه داری

Valikan key nomaaee rokh be rendaan

To kaz khorshido mah aaeene daari

ولیکن کی نمائی رخ به رندان

تو کز خورشید و مه آیینه داری

Bade rendaan magoo ey sheikh hosh daar

Ke baa mehre khodaaee kine daari

بد رندان مگو ای شیخ و هش دار

که با مهرخدائی کینه داری

Nemitarsi ze aahe aatashinam

To daani khergheye pashmina daari

نمی ترسی ز آه آتشینم

تو دانی خرقه پشمینه داری

Nadidam khosh tar az shere to Hafez

Be ghoraani ke andar sine daari

ندیدم خوشتر از شعر تو حافظ

به قرآنی که اندر سینه داری

In my eye one who has a moon-like eyebrow, there is,
Of one with fresh down, somewhere a drawn image there is.

The reins of this dervish's heart have been given to one,
Who cares not at all for the crown and throne of anyone.

My head is out of my control, my eye has been burnt in waiting,
Longing for the head and eye of one who decorates the gathering.

It's an amazing notion that the permission for my love play,
From a petite eyebrow is signed off in such full blown way.

My heart is dark; I will set on fire the robe of the Sufi,
Come and see, I am sure a grand show it will prove to be.

On that eventful day make my coffin from the tall cypress tree,
We will go as one bearing the burned mark of one who is lofty.

At that stage where beautiful ones draw the sword of glance-giving,
To see a head that on to a foot has fallen should not be so surprising.

Separation and union - so what? What the friend wishes, seek to do[1],
To desire anything other than that one, would be a sad thing to do.

When that one's face has put the moon in my night chamber,
To a twinkling star how should I give any attention whatever?

The fish would bring pearls to scatter with great liberality,
If the ship of Hafiz's verse you were to launch on the sea.

(W-C 519) The radif here translates into many different terms such as "a place"; "a foot"; "a spectacle".
   [1] *"..What the friend wishes, seek to do..." One is reminded of accounts of Hazrat Abu Said Abi'l Khair, of a saint who was dying. Someone at his bedside said – "I know you are never forgetful of Allah even for a single moment. The dying man replied he wanted to always be doing the Will of Allah even if it meant not remembering Him. See pp. 20 in the introduction to "Abu Said Abi'l Khair and his Rubaiyat" by Dr Z. H. Sharib. Sharib Press; Southampton.1992.*

Be chashm kardeam abrooye maah simaaee
Khiyaale sabz khati naghsh basteam jaaee

به چشم کرده ام ابروی ماه سیمایی
خیال سبز خطی نقش بسته ام جایی

Zamaame del be kasi daadeam mane darvish
Ke nistash be kas az taajo takht parvaaee

زمام دل به کسی داده ام من درویش
که نیستش به کس از تاج و تخت پروایی

Saram ze dast beshod chashm az entezaar besookht
Dar aarezooye saro chashme majles aaraaee

سرم ز دست بشد چشم از انتظار بسوخت
در آرزوی سر و چشم مجلس آرایی

Zehi khiyaal ke manshoore eshgh baaziye man
Aaz aan kamaancheye abroo rasad be toghraaee

زهی خیال که منشور عشقبازی من
از آن کمانچه ابرو رسد به طغرایی

Mokaddar ast del aatash be kherghe khaaham zad
Biyaa bebin ke keraa mikonad tamaashaaee

مکدّر است دل آتش به خرقه خواهم زد
بیا ببین که کرا می کند تماشایی

Be rooze vaaghe e taaboote maa ze sarv konid
Ke miravim be daaghe boland baalaaee

به روز واقعه تابوت ما ز سرو کنید
که می رویم به داغ بلند بالایی

Dar aan maghaam ke khoobaan ze ghamze tigh kashand
Ajab madaar sari ooftaade dar paaee

در آن مقام که خوبان ز غمزه تیغ کشند
عجب مدار سری اوفتاده در پایی

Feraagho vasl che baashad rezaaye doost talab
Ke heyf baashad azoo gheyre ou taman naaee

فراق و وصل چه باشد رضای دوست طلب
که حیف باشد ازو غیر او تمنّایی

Maraa ke az rokhe ou maah dar shabestaan ast
Kojaa bovad be forooghe setaare parvaaee

مرا که از رخ او ماه در شبستان است
کجا بود به فروغ ستاره پروایی

Dorar ze shovgh bar aarand maahiyaan be nesaar
Agar safineye Hafez bari be daryaaee

درر ز شوق برآرند ماهیان به نثار
اگر سفینه حافظ بری به دریایی

By your very life I swear, if my life were mine to give,
The least of your slave's offerings it would have been.

If my heart had not been caught in the curl of your hair,
The power to endure this dark dust-pit could there have been?

Like the sun on the horizon of every sky, singular is your face,
Oh dear, if only in that heart a particle of kindness there had been.

I would speak of the price of the dust under your foot,
If only for precious life an eternity there had been.

O that like a beam of light you had streamed in by my door,
So that both my eyes flowing under your command had been.

The cypress would have declared slavery to your stature,
If in it, like the noble lily, ten tongues there had been.

How could Hafiz's wailing have emerged from the veil,
If one of the birds of the dawn chorus he had not been.

(W-C 520) The radif here translates into several terms such as "Would have been"; "Should have been".
We have used variations on "Have been" as the only rhyme.

Be jaane ou ke garam dastras be jaan boodi
Kamine pish keshe bandegaansh aan boodi

به جان او که گرم دسترس به جان بودی
کمینه پیشکش بندگانش آن بودی

Agar delam nashodi paay bande torreye ou
Keyam gharaar darin tire khaak daan boodi

اگر دلم نشدی پای بند طرّه او
کی ام قرار درین تیره خاکدان بودی

Be rokh cho mehre falak bi nazire aafaagh ast
Be del darigh ke yek zarre mehrabaan boodi

به رخ چو مهر فلک بی نظیر آفاق است
به دل دریغ که یک ذرّه مهربان بودی

Begoftami ke bahaa chist khaake paayash raa
Agar hayaate geraan maaye jaavdaan boodi

بگفتمی که بها چیست خاک پایش را
اگر حیات گرانمایه جاودان بودی

Daraamadi ze daram kaajki cho lam e ye noor
Ke bar do dideye maa hokme ou ravaan boodi

درآمدی ز درم کاجکی چو لمعه نور
که بر دو دیده ما حکم او روان بودی

Be bandegiyye ghadash sarv mo taref gashti
Garash cho soosane aazaade dah zabaan boodi

به بندگیّ قدش سرو معترف گشتی
گرش چو سوسن آزاده ده زبان بودی

Ze parde naaleye Hafez boroon key oftaadi
Agar na hamdame morghaane sobh khaan boodi

ز پرده ناله حافظ برون کی افتادی
اگر نه همدم مرغان صبح خوان بودی

How would it have been if the heart of that beloved had been kind?
If it had been so, our state would not have been of this or that kind.

If these days of ours had held me in respect and had cherished me,
Dust on that one's doorstep would have been a seat of honour to me.

Let alone having union, the beloved in dreams I do not see!
That being so, I would to God that this other there would be.

The cost of the wind from the beloved's curls would have been told by me,
If for every hair tip of mine a thousand lifetimes there had happened to be.

Lord how would it have been less, if on the Order for our heart's joy,
The stamp of "Safety from time's disasters" you had chosen to employ?

I wish from the veil, like a teardrop, the beloved would have come,
So that under your command both my flowing eyes would have come.

The circle of love would close the way, if it had not been like this,
At its centre point would have been the heart-bewildered Hafiz.

(W-C 521) The radif here is mostly "Would have been".

Che boodi ar dele aan yaar mehrbaan boodi
Ke haale maa na chonin boodi ar chonaan boodi

Garam zamaane sarafraaz daashtiyyo aziz
Sarire ezzatam aan khaake aastaan boodi

Be khaab niz nemibinamash che jaaye vesaal
Cho in naboodo nadidim baari aan boodi

Begoftami ke che arzad nasime torreye doost
Garam be har sare mooee hezaar jaan boodi

Baraate khosh deliye maa che kam shodi yaa rab
Garash neshaane amaan az bade zamaan boodi

Ze parde kaaj boroon aamadi cho ghatreye ashk
Ke bar do dideye maa hokme ou ravaan boodi

Agar na daayereye eshgh raah bar basti
Cho noghte Hafeze sargashte dar miyaan boodi

چه بودی ار دل آن یار مهربان بودی
که حال ما نه چنین بودی ار چنان بودی

گرم زمانه سرافراز داشتیّ و عزیز
سریر عزّتم آن خاک آستان بودی

به خواب نیز نمی بینمش چه جای وصال
چو این نبود و ندیدیم باری آن بودی

بگفتمی که چه ارزد نسیم طرّه دوست
گرم به هر سر موئی هزار جان بودی

برات خوشدلی ما چه کم شدی یا رب
گرش نشان امان از بد زمان بودی

ز پرده کاج برون آمدی چو قطره اشک
که بر دو دیده ما حکم او روان بودی

اگر نه دایره عشق راه بر بستی
چو نقطه حافظ سرگشته در میان بودی

If you are sitting at the edge of a stream full of self- illusion,
Then any calamity you may see arises from your own delusion[1].

By God, Who has chosen you to be a servant,
Don't prefer any other to this ancient servant.

Polite deference made a monarch of beauty out of you,
Well done, more is deserved a hundred times over by you.

If not enduring patiently your guardian's tyranny,
To be wretched and humble is the lover's only remedy.

Rose, I wonder at your graciousness to sit with the thorn as you do,
Maybe at this present moment this appears expedient to you.

If I hold securely on to my integrity there is no cause for worry,
The heart's surrender is easy enough, if it lead not to infidelity.

Hear a word from a slave, who is unbiased and sincere,
You, who are the focus of attention for every truth seer.

If you sauntered towards the garden it would seem a pity to me,
For you are fresher the than rose and jonquil, and more lovely.

The bubble in the glass of my tear, from left and right is seen,
If you pause in the place where visions are to be seen.

For one with your pure heart and abstinent tendency,
With men of evil nature better not to keep company.

The flood of tears washed away patience from the heart of Hafiz,
O pupil of my eye don't desert me, too much it is to endure this.

O you delicate natured, heart-seducing source of teasing,
The banquet hall of Khwaja Jalaluddin[2] you are deserving.

(W-C 522)

[1] "...verse one would seem to imply that the beloved should not sit at the edge of a stream where they can see their own reflection or it will cause commotion from the beloved's beauty. We have put an alternate version in the appendix.

[2] "...Khwaja Jalaluddin..." This is thought to refer to Khwaja (Maulana) Jalaluddin Rumi (d.1273) who is buried in Konya. He founded the Mevlevi Order and is the author of the great Masnevi and numerous other writings.

To magar bar labe aabi be havas ben shini
Var na har fetne ke bini hame az khod bini

تو مگر بر لب آبی به هوس بنشینی
ورنه هر فتنه که بینی همه از خود بینی

Be khodaaee ke toee bandeye bogzideye ou
Ke barin chaakere dirine kasi nagzini

به خدائی که توئی بنده بگزیده او
که بر این چاکر دیرینه کسی نگزینی

Adabo sharm to raa khosrove mahrooyaan kard
Aafarin bar to ke shaayesteye sad chandini

ادب و شرم تو را خسرو مهرویان کرد
آفرین بر تو که شایسته صد چندینی

Sabr bar jovre raghibat che konam gar nakonam
Aasheghaan raa nabovad chaare bejoz meskini

صبر بر جور رقیبت چکنم گر نکنم
عاشقان را نبود چاره بجز مسکینی

Ajab az lotfe to ey gol ke neshini baa khaar
Zaaheran maslahate vaght daraan mibini

عجب از لطف تو ای گل که نشینی با خار
ظاهراً مصلحت وقت در آن می بینی

Gar amaanat be salaamat bebaram baaki nist
Bi deli sahl agar az pey nabovad bi dini

گر امانت به سلامت ببرم باکی نیست
بی دلی سهل اگر از پی نبود بی دینی

Sokhane bigharaz az bandeye mokhles besheno
Ey ke manzoore bozorgaane haghighat bini

سخن بی غرض از بنده مخلص بشنو
ای که منظور بزرگان حقیقت بینی

Heyfam aayad ke kharaami be tamaashaaye chaman
Ke to khoshtar ze golo taaze taraz nasrini

حیفم آید که خرامی به تماشای چمن
که تو خوشتر ز گل و تازه تر از نسرینی

Shishe baaziyye sereshkam negari az chapo raast
gar barin manzare binesh nafasi benshini

شیشه بازیِّ سرشکم نگری از چپ و راست
گر برین منظر بینش نفسی بنشینی

Paarsaaee cho to paakize dele paak nahaad
Behtar aan ast ke baa mardome bad nanshini

پارسایی چو تو پاکیزه دل پاک نهاد
بهتر آن است که با مردم بد ننشینی

Seyle in ashke ravaan sabre dele Hafez bord
Balaghat taaghato yaa moghlata ayni bayni

سیل این اشک روان صبر دل حافظ برد
بلغ الطاقه یا مقله عینی بینی

To bedin naazokiyo delkashi ey maayeye naaz
Laayeghe bazm gahe khaaje jalaaleddini

تو بدین نازکی و دلکشی ای مایه ناز
لایق بزمگه خواجه جلال الدّینی

On the day of trial[1] good support the revolving sphere was giving,
So how will you show gratitude? What gift will you be giving?

In love's street they don't buy the trappings of royalty,
Confess to your servitude and demonstrate your slavery.

As one who has fallen but whose hand God has taken,
May sympathy fall on you for the suffering of the fallen.

With good news of joy come in through my door, O Saki,
So lifted for a moment from my heart worldly woes may be.

On the highway of prestige and pomp is much danger,
Travel light through this pass; to be unburdened, is better.

The King has worries for the army, the crown, and the treasure;
The Dervish has peace of mind and the roaming mystic's corner.

If you will permit, I offer the words of a single Sufi saying?
"O light of my eye – peace is better than war and empire building".

Attentiveness and concentrated firm resolve[2] brings what is desired,
From the king resolve to be charitable and from God what is needed.

From your face don't wash the dust of contentment and poverty,
For, O Hafiz, this dust is better than the work of alchemy.

(W-C 523)
[1] "...On the day of trial..." W-C translates this as The Day of Judgement but Saberi translates it as day of war, and Avery as the day of trial. These latter are much more plausible.
[2] "...concentrated firm resolve..." Fikr and Himmat. See in the glossary in volume one for Himmat. Fikr is consciousness of the Divine in thought, feeling and action.

Khosh kard yaavari falakat rooze daavari

خوش کرد یاوری فلکت روز داوری

Taa shokr chon koniyyo che shokraane aavari

تا شکر چون کنیّ و چه شکرانه آوری

Dar kooye eshgh shovkate shaahi nemikharand

در کوی عشق شوکت شاهی نمی خرند

Eghraare bandegi kono ezhaare chaakeri

اقرار بندگی کن و اظهار چاکری

Aankas ke ooftaado khodaayash gereft dast

آنکس که اوفتاد و خدایش گرفت دست

Goo bar to baad taa ghame oftaadegaan khori

گو بر تو باد تا غم افتادگان خوری

Saaghi be mojdegaaniye eysh az daram daraay

ساقی به مژدگانی عیش از درم درآی

Taa yek damaz delam ghame donyaa be dar bari

تا یکدم از دلم غم دنیا به در بری

Dar shaah raahe jaaho bozorgi khatar basist

در شاهراه جاه و بزرگی خطر بسیست

Aan beh kazin garive sabok baar bogzari

آن به کزین گریوه سبکبار بگذری

Soltaano fekre lashkaro sovdaaye ganjo taaj

سلطان و فکر لشکر و سودای گنج و تاج

Darvisho amne khaatero konje ghalandari

درویش و امن خاطر و کنج قلندری

Yek harfe soofiyaane begooyam ejaazat ast

یک حرف صوفیانه بگویم اجازت است

Ey noore dide solh behaz jango daavari

ای نور دیده صلح به از جنگ و داوری

Neyle moraad bar hasabe fekro hemmat ast

نیل مراد بر حسب فکر و همّت است

Az shaah nazre kheyro ze tovfigh yaavari

از شاه نذر خیر و ز توفیق یاوری

Hafez ghobaare faghro ghanaa-at ze rokh mashooy

حافظ غبار فقر و قناعت ز رخ مشوی

Kin khaak behtar az amale kimiyaa gari

کاین خاک بهتر از عمل کیمیا گری

Two[1] sensitive friends, matured wine in two large measures,
A good book, a garden nook, and time for these pleasures.

For this or the next world I wouldn't give up this state of being
Though at every moment around me followers are gathering.

Whoever gave up contentment's corner for the world's treasure,
Has sold Yusuf of Egypt[2] for a price that is extremely meagre.

Come! This workshop won't lose profit nor will it be less busy,
Due to the ascetic piety of the likes of you, or my debauchery.

See in the mirror of the cup the artistry of the world unseen,
No one can recall when such an amazing thing there has been.

With the hot blast of winds that over the garden blew fiercely,
Wonderful, if a trace of rose's scent or jasmine's colour there be.

Be patient O heart for Truth does not allow for very long,
That such a seal-ring[3] to the hand of an evil one belong.

In this disaster the very composition of the universe was ruined, Hafiz,
What does the doctor think? Say what the judgment of the Brahmin is[4].

(W-C 524) The radif here translates into many different terms such as "a corner"; "a crowd"; "a very paltry sum".
[1] *The first verse speaks of two friends, two measures of wine and there is a repetition of two throughout the ghazal. One is reminded of the frequent reference to two, in Sura Rehman in the holy Qur'an. There is also a reference to a mirror in verse five where the real and the reflected exist as both two and one. Perhaps this is because the physical universe is seen as a reflection of Allah.*
[2] *"..sold Yusuf of Egypt..." A reference to Prophet Joseph who was sold in the market place as a slave – see Sura Yusuf in the holy Qur'an.*
[3] *"..That such a seal ring..."This is at one level a reference to the story of Prophet Solomon (Suleiman) whose Kingdom was briefly usurped by a devil by means of the theft of his seal ring. It is also suggested by translators that this refers also to a time in the history of Shiraz when it was taken temporarily by Tamerlane but later passed to by him to Shah Yahya.*
[4] *"..the last line also has a reference to two – invoking both the wisdom of a doctor and a Brahmin (an upper caste Hindu), here probably used to signify a learned man.*

Do yaare naazoko az baadeye kohan do mani
Faraaghatiyyo ketaabiyyo goosheye chamani

دو یار نازک و از باده کهن دو منی
فراغتیّ و کتابیّ و گوشه چمنی

Man in maghaam be donyaavo aakherat nadaham
Agarche dar peyam oftand har dam anjomani

من این مقام به دنیا و آخرت ندهم
اگرچه در پی ام افتند هر دم انجمنی

Ke harke konje ghanaa-at be ganje donyaa daad
Forookht yoosofe mesri be kamtarin samani

که هر که کنج قناعت به گنج دنیا داد
فروخت یوسف مصری به کمترین ثمنی

Biyaa ke foshate in kaarkhaane kam nashavad
Be zohde hamcho toee yaa be fesghe hamcho mani

بیا که فسحت این کارخانه کم نشود
به زهد همچو توئی یا به فسق همچو منی

Bebin daraayeneye jaam naghshbandiye gheyb
Ke kas be yaad nadaarad chonin ajab zamani

ببین در آینه جام نقشبندی غیب
که کس به یاد ندارد چنین عجب زمنی

Azin samoom ke bar tarfe boostaan bogzasht
Ajab ke booye goli hasto range yaasamani

ازین سموم که بر طرف بوستان بگذشت
عجب که بوی گلی هست و رنگ یاسمنی

Be sabr koosh to ey del ke hagh rahaa nakonad
Chonin aziz negini be daste ahremani

به صبر کوش تو ای دل که حق رها نکند
چنین عزیز نگینی به دست اهرمنی

Mezaaje dahr tabah shod darin balaa Hafez
Kojaast fekre hakimiyyo raaye barhamani

مزاج دهر تبه شد درین بلا حافظ
کجاست فکر حکیمیّ و رای برهمنی

There is none as crazy as me in all the Magian[1] precincts put together,
My dervish robe is in hock for wine in one place, my book in another.

The royal mirror of my heart is clouded over and dusty,
I ask of God the company of one who sees more clearly.

I took an oath of repentance at the hand of a wine-selling beauty,
To drink no wine if the face of a party-pleasing idol I couldn't see.

From the eye to my robe I have let streams flow freely,
So that they might place near me a cypress-like beauty.

The ship-shaped cup of wine bring! The friend's face being missing,
Each corner of my eye has become entirely an ocean of grieving.

Maybe, the tongue of the candle can tell this secret's subtlety,
Otherwise, with words, the moth not at all interested will be.

Don't feel bad if the narcissus boasts of an eye of beauty,
The clear-sighted won't go after one who cannot see.

I am the beloved's worshipper; don't mention another to me!
Other than that one and the cup of wine, nothing interests me.

It was very good to hear this exposition in the early morning,
With pipe and drum at the tavern's door by one who is God-fearing;

"If to be a Muslim is to be as this Hafiz is,
Oh dear, what if after today a tomorrow[2] there is."

(W-C 525)

[1] "...Magian..." See glossary in volume one.
[2] 'Tomorrow' usually refers to The Day of Judgement. The story told by Avery and mentioned by W-C is that the penultimate verse was inserted later. The reason being that a fatwa, a religious edict, was issued because it appeared that in the last verse Hafiz was casting doubt on the The Day of Judgement, which is an article of faith for Muslims. According to the story these words were therefore made to appear as being quoted from a Christian. See Avery pp. 584.

Dar hame deyre moghaan nist cho man sheydaaee
Kherghe jaaee gerove baadevo daftar jaaee

Del ke aaeeneye shaahist ghobaari daarad
Az khodaa mitalabam sohbate rovshan raaee

Kardeam tovbe be daste sanami baade foroosh
Ke degar mey nakhoram bi rokhe bazm aaraaee

Jooy haa basteam az dide be daaman ke magar
Bar kenaaram beneshaanand sahi baalaaee

Kashtiye baade biyaavar ke maraa bi rokhe doost
Gasht har goosheye chashm az ghame del daryaaee

Serre in nokte magar sha-m baraarad be zabaan
Var na parvaane nadaarad be sokhan parvaaee

Narges ar laaf zad az shiveye chashme to maranj
Naravand ahle nazar az peye naabinaaee

Sokhane gheyr magoo baa mane ma-shooghe parast
Kaz veyo jaame meyam nist be kas parvaaee

In hadisam che khosh aamad ke sahar gah migoft
Bar dare meykadei baa dafo ney tarsaaee

Gar mosalmaani az in ast ke Hafez daarad
Aah agar az peye emrooz bovad fardaaee

در همه دیر مغان نیست چو من شیدایی
خرقه جایی گرو باده و دفتر جایی

دل که آیینه شاهیست غباری دارد
از خدا می طلبم صحبت روشن رایی

کرده ام توبه به دست صنمی باده فروش
که دگر می نخورم بی رخ بزم آرایی

جوی ها بسته ام از دیده به دامن که مگر
برکنارم بنشانند سهی بالایی

کشتی باده بیاور که مرا بی رخ دوست
گشت هر گوشه چشم از غم دل دریایی

سرّ این نکته مگر شمع برآرد به زبان
ورنه پروانه ندارد به سخن پروایی

نرگس ار لاف زد از شیوه چشم تو مرنج
نروند اهل نظر از پی نابینایی

سخن غیر مگو با من معشوقه پرست
کز وی و جام می ام نیست به کس پروایی

این حدیثم چه خوش آمد که سحرگه می گفت
بردر میکده ای با دف و نی ترسایی

گر مسلمانی از این است که حافظ دارد
آه اگر از پی امروز بود فردایی

Last night in dream I saw that a great moon had appeared,
Reflected in its face I saw that separation had disappeared.

What is the meaning? The return of my friend the traveler;
I wish that one had been able to come to my door sooner.

May my fortune-favoured Saki's name be recalled fondly,
With goblet and cup he would come through my door frequently.

It would be good if in dream he saw his native city,
So that, recollecting friendship, he would come to me.

If the bounty of Azal[1] could be got by force or gold,
The water of Khizr[2], Alexander would have come to hold.

Remember fondly the time when 'from roof and door'[3], to me,
From the beloved a message or letter would come constantly.

How would your guardian have continued to abuse power so long,
If to the ruler's gate one night a victim of tyranny had come along.

Those who have never walked the path know what of love's flavour?
Seek one whose heart is an ocean and famous for brave behaviour.

That one who showed the path of stony heartedness to you,
I wish his feet had come into collision with a hard rock too.

If any other person had written in Hafiz's style and manner,
With the art patronising king he would have come into favour.

(W-C 526) The radif here translates into slightly different terms such as "Had come"; "Used to come";
"Would have come".
   [1] *"...Azal..." The Day of pre-eternity, Alast.*
   [2] *"...Khizr..." See glossary in volume one.*
   [3] *"...from roof and door..." From every quarter.*

Didam be khaab doosh ke maahi baraamadi
Kaz akse rooye ou shabe hejraan saraamadi

دیدم به خواب دوش که ماهی برآمدی
کز عکس روی او شب هجران سر آمدی

Ta-bir chist yaare safar karde miresad
Ey kaaj har che zoodtar az dar daraamadi

تعبیر چیست یار سفر کرده می رسد
ای کاج هر چه زودتر از در درآمدی

Zekrash be kheyr saaghiye farkhonde faale man
Kaz dar modaam baa ghadaho saaghar aamadi

ذکرش به خیر ساقی فرخنده فال من
کز در مدام با قدح و ساغرآمدی

Khosh boodi ar be khaab bedidi diyaare khish
Taa yaade sohbatash sooye maa rahbar aamadi

خوش بودی ار به خواب بدیدی دیار خویش
تا یاد صحبتش سوی ما رهبر آمدی

Feyze azal be zooro zar ar aamadi be dast
Aabe khezer nasibeye eskandar aamadi

فیض ازل به زور و زر ار آمدی به دست
آب خضر نصیبه اسکندر آمدی

Aan ahd yaad baad ke az baamo dar maraa
Har dam payaame yaaro khate delbar aamadi

آن عهد یاد باد که از بام و در مرا
هر دم پیام یار و خط دلبر آمدی

Key yaafti raghibe to chandin majaale zolm
Mazloomi ar shabi be dare daavar aamadi

کی یافتی رقیب تو چندین مجال ظلم
مظلومی ار شبی به در داور آمدی

Khaamaane rah narafte che daanand zovghe eshgh
Daryaa deli bejooy daliri saraamadi

خامان ره نرفته چه دانند ذوق عشق
دریا دلی بجوی دلیری سر آمدی

Aankoo toraa be sangdeli kard rah nomoon
Ey kaashki ke paash be sangi baraamadi

آنکاو ترا به سنگدلی کرد رهنمون
ای کاشکی که پاش به سنگی بر آمدی

Gar digari be shiveye Hafez zadi ragham
Maghboole tab-e shaahe honar parvar aamadi

گر دیگری به شیوه حافظ زدی قلم
مقبول طبع شاه هنرپرور آمدی

You have kept us fretting with expectations for a long while,
Others you care for, but you keep the sincere ones in this style.

You have not opened even a corner of the eye of satisfaction,
Is this how you give honour to those endowed with vision?

Since to rose and bulbul the dawn breeze read the page of your beauty,
You have kept them all busy screaming and destroying their finery.

Best you cover your forearm, since for the purpose of painting on it,
In the hearts' blood of those with talent, your hand is kept dipped.

You, who from those patched coat wearers, seek the flavour of Presence,
It's strange to seek an eye for mysteries from those with no such sense.

O eye and lamp! As you are the narcissus[1] of the garden of perception,
Why do you keep this heart-sore and hurt one without your attention.

The essence of Jamshid's cup is a jewel mined in another place,
Yet it's in the clay of the potter you keep desiring to find its trace.

Heart, you are the father of experience, then how should it be,
That you keep on expecting from your sons love and fidelity.

Though our Rend way and ruination is our own sinful action,
A lover said, "It is you who keep your slave in this situation".

Hafiz, on the day of peace and safety do not be complaining,
From such a fleeting world what expectation are you keeping?

(W-C 527) The radif here is "You keep".
[1] "...narcissus..." the orange corona (cup) of some kinds of the narcissus flower may easily look like an eye to the imagination.

Rooze gaarist ke maa raa negaraan midaari
Mokhlesaan raa na be vaz-e degaraan midaari

روزگاریست که ما را نگران می داری
مخلصان را نه به وضع دگران می داری

Goosheye chashme rezaaee be manat baaz nashod
In chonin ezzate saaheb nazaraan midaari

گوشه چشم رضائ‌ی به منت باز نشد
این چنین عزّت صاحب نظران می داری

Taa sabaa bar golo bolbol varaghe hosne to khaand
Hame raa na-rezanaan jaame daraan midaari

تا صبا بر گل و بلبل ورق حسن تو خواند
همه را نعره زنان جامه دران می داری

Saaed aan beh ke bepooshi to cho az bahre negaar
Dast dar khoone dele por honaraan midaari

ساعد آن به که بپوشی تو چو از بهر نگار
دست در خون دل پرهنران می داری

Ey ke dar dalghe molamma talabi zovghe hozoor
Chashme serri ajab az bi khabaraan midaari

ای که در دلق ملمّع طلبی ذوق حضور
چشم سری عجب از بی خبران می داری

Nargese baaghe nazar chon toaee ey chashmo cheraagh
Sar cheraa bar mane del khaste geraan midaari

نرگس باغ نظر چون توئی ای چشم و چراغ
سر چرا بر من دلخسته گران می داری

Govhare jaame jam az kaane jahaani degar ast
To tamannaa ze gele kooze garaan midaari

گوهر جام جم از کان جهانی دگر است
تو تمنّا ز گل کوزه گران می داری

Pedare tajrobe ey del toee aakher ze che rooy
Ta-mae mehro vafaa zin pesaraan midaari

پدر تجربه ای دل توئی آخر ز چه روی
طمع مهر و وفا زین پسران می داری

Garche rendiyyo kharaabi gonahe maast hame
Aasheghi goft ke to bande bar aan midaari

گرچه رندیّ و خرابی گنه ماست همه
عاشقی گفت که تو بنده بر آن می داری

Magzaraan rooze salaamat be malaamat Hafez
Che tavagh gho ze jahaane gozaraan midaari

مگذران روز سلامت به ملامت حافظ
چه توقّع ز جهان گذران می داری

I went in the garden to pick a rose, one morning,
Suddenly to my ear came the bulbul's singing.

The poor dear was caught up in love for the rose, like me,
And throughout the garden was sending his plaintive plea.

All the time whilst round the lawn and garden strolling,
About the rose and bulbul I was busy in meditating.

The rose befriended beauty; the bulbul became love's companion;
Nothing changed for the one, in the other there was no alteration.

Since the bulbul's song had roused my heart so deeply,
I had become one who could not bear anything patiently.

Though in this garden many roses will be blooming, yet,
Anyone who gathers a rose, a thorn's sting will also get.

From the turning of the world expect nothing, Hafiz,
In it are a thousand flaws but not a single virtue there is.

(W-C 528) The radif here translates into different terms such as "A rose"; "A clamour"; "A change".

Raftam be baagh sobh dami taa chenam goli

Aamad be goosh naagaham aavaaze bolboli

رفتم به باغ صبحدمی تا چنم گلی

آمد به گوش ناگهم آواز بلبلی

Meskin cho man be eshghe goli gashte mobtalaa

Vandar chaman fekande ze faryaad gholgholi

مسکین چو من به عشق گلی گشته مبتلا

واندر چمن فکنده ز فریاد غلغلی

Migashtam andar aan chamano baagh dam be dam

Mikardam andar aan golo bolbol ta-ammoli

می گشتم اندر آن چمن و باغ دمبدم

می کردم اندر آن گل و بلبل تأملی

Gol yaare hosn gashtevo bolbol gharine eshgh

In raa taghayyori nevo aan raa tabaddoli

گل یار حسن گشته و بلبل قرین عشق

این را تغیّری نه و آن را تبدّلی

Chon kard dar delam asar aavaaze andalib

Gashtam chonaan ke hich namaandam tahammoli

چون کرد در دلم اثر آواز عندلیب

گشتم چنانکه هیچ نماندم تحمّلی

Bas gol shekofte mishavad in baagh raa vali

Kas bi balaaye khaar nachidast azoo goli

بس گل شکفته می شود این باغ را ولی

کس بی بلای خار نچیده ست ازو گلی

Hafez madaar omide faraj zin madaare kovn

Daarad hezaar eybo nadaarad tafazzoli

حافظ مدار امید فرج زین مدار کون

دارد هزار عیب و ندارد تفضّلی

When on your rose cheek this line of beauty is drawn by you
The page of the rose and rose garden is crossed out by you.

The tears that much prefer to remain in my inner sanctuary,
From behind seven veils you draw into a place of publicity.

By the scent of your hair the lazy pace of the breeze of dawn,
With the chains of your hair, sweetly into busy activity is drawn.

The memory of your wine-coloured lip and drunken eye, ever,
Draw me from a secluded place to the house of the wine-seller.

You told me that tied to your saddle pack my head should be,
I said, "If you can draw this heavy load along that's fine by me".

Expected to cope with your eye and eyebrow, how can this heart be?
Oh dear - this bow that you draw against a suffering one like me.

I will keep the evil eye away from your cheek, come back,
O fresh rose, whose skirt from this thorn is drawn back.

 O Hafiz, what else is it you want from what this sphere is offering?
You drink wine and the loved one's hair into your hand are drawing.

(W-C 529) The radif here is "You draw".

In khosh ragham ke bar gole rokhsaar mikeshi
Khat bar sahifeye golo golzaar mikeshi

اين خوش رقم که بر گل رخسار می کشی
خط بر صحيفه گل و گلزار می کشی

Ashke haram neshine nahaan khaaneye maraa
Zaan sooye haft parde be baazaar mikeshi

اشک حرم نشين نهانخانه مرا
زان سوی هفت پرده به بازار می کشی

Kaahel rovi cho baade sabaa raa be booye zolf
Shirin be gheydo selsele dar kaar mikeshi

کاهل روی چو باد صبا را به بوی زلف
شيرين به قيد و سلسله در کار می کشی

Har dam be yaade aan labe meygoono chashme mast
Az khalvatam be khaaneye khammaar mikeshi

هر دم به ياد آن لب ميگون و چشم مست
از خلوتم به خانه خمّار می کشی

Gofti sare to basteye fetraake maa shavad
sahl ast agar to zahmate in baar mikeshi

گفتی سر تو بسته فتراک ما شود
سهل است اگر تو زحمت اين بار می کشی

Baa chashmo abrooye to che tadbire del konam
Vah zin kamaan ke bar mane bimaar mikeshi

با چشم و ابروی تو چه تدبير دل کنم
وه زين کمان که بر من بيمار می کشی

Baazaa ke chashme bad ze rokhat da-f mikonam
Ey taaze gol ke daaman azin khaar mikeshi

باز آ که چشم بد ز رخت دفع می کنم
ای تازه گل که دامن ازين خار می کشی

Hafez degar che mitalabi az naeeme dahr
Mey micheshiyyo torreye deldaar mikeshi

حافظ دگر چه می طلبی از نعيم دهر
می می چشيّ و طرّه دلدار می کشی

Who will bring from my heart-stealer the pen's kindness to me?
Where is that courier breeze, if he is still inclined toward mercy?

For the intellect's approach to love's path I made this analogy,
It is like a dew drop trying to make an impression on the sea.

Come, for though with the Sufi robe of mine taverns I endow,
No charitable foundation has on record that me they did endow.

Why don't they buy for the price of only one sugar reed Ney,
One who pours out a hundred sweetness's from the pen's Ney.

From under a rug beating my drum - my heart fled this hypocrisy,
Its better that at the tavern door my standard I am raising boldly.

Come, they sell both worlds[2] who know time's mystery,
For just one cup of pure wine and the company of a beauty.

The way of love is not an easy one or continuously pleasing,
If you want our company drink the poison of much grieving.

The doctor who sits besides the way, love's pain he knows not,
You with a dead heart, find one who the Messiah's breath has got.

I don't complain at all, but from the friend's cloud of mercy,
Not a drop came to the land of those whose livers are thirsty.

O heart, thinking how and why leads to head hurting,
Take a cup and for a moment in your life be resting.

O King, Hafiz has nothing in his hand at all worthy of you,
Other than nightly pleading and morning supplication too.

(W-C 530) The radif here translates into different terms such as "A kindness"; "A mark" & etc.
[1] "...one who pours..." This implies of course Hafiz himself. Why buy a product when you can have the maker of the product.
[2] "...both the worlds..." This material existence and the life after death. Eternal union with the Divine Beloved is their only concern.

Ze delbaram ke resaanad navaazeshe ghalami

Kojaast peyke sabaa gar hami konad karami

ز دلبرم که رساند نوازش قلمی

کجاست پیک صبا گر همی کند کرمی

Ghiyaas kardamo tadbire aghl dar rahe eshgh

Cho shabnamist ke bar bahr mikeshad raghami

قیاس کردم و تدبیر عقل در ره عشق

چو شبنمیست که بر بحر می کشد رقمی

Biyaa ke khergheye man garche rahne meykadehaast

Ze maale vaghf nabini be naame man derami

بیا که خرقه من گرچه رهن میکده هاست

ز مال وقف نبینی به نام من درمی

Cheraa be yek neye ghandash nemikharand aan kas

Ke kard sad shekar afshaani az neye ghalami

چرا به یک نی قندش نمی خرند آن کس

که کرد صد شکر افشانی از نی قلمی

Delam gereft ze saalooso table zire gelim

Beh aan ke bar dare meykhaane bar konam alami

دلم گرفت ز سالوس و طبل زیر گلیم

به آنکه بر در میخانه بر کنم علمی

Biyaa ke vaght shenaasaan do kovn befrooshand

Be yek piyaale meye saafo sohbate sanami

بیا که وقت شناسان دو کون بفروشند

به یک پیاله می صاف و صحبت صنمی

Davaame eysho tanaom na shiveye eshgh ast

Agar moaashere maaee benoosh nishe ghami

دوام عیش و تنعّم نه شیوه عشق است

اگر معاشر مائی بنوش نیش غمی

Tabibe raah neshin darde eshgh nash naasad

Boro be dast kon ey morde del masih dami

طبیب راه نشین درد عشق نشناسد

برو به دست کن ای مرده دل مسیح دمی

Nemikonam gelei liken abre rahmate doost

Be kesht zaare jegar tesh negaan nadaad name

نمی کنم گله ای لیکن ابر رحمت دوست

به کشتزار جگرتشنگان نداد نمی

Hadise choono cheraa darde sar dahad ey del

Piyaale giro biyaasaa ze omre khish dami

حدیث چون و چرا دردسر دهد ای دل

پیاله گیر و بیاسا ز عمر خویش دمی

Sezaaye ghadre to shaahaa be daste Hafez nist

Joz az doaaye shabiyyo niyaaze sobh dami

سزای قدر تو شاها به دست حافظ نیست

جز از دعای شبی و نیاز صبحدمی

From the street of the beloved comes the New Year's breeze[1],
Light a lamp in your heart if you want help from this breeze.

If, like the rose, you hold gold spend it, for God's sake, on pleasure,
For Karun[2] was really brought down by his desire for storing treasure.

From within the veil my word is, burst from the bud like a rose,
For the rule of the lord of the New Year[3] only for five days goes.

I have wine that has soul like purity, yet the Sufi is not glad,
O God, even for a day let no wise man have luck that's bad.

What is the way of joy, to abandon wanting it,
Your own crown's border you sew by doing it.

I don't know why the turtle dove by the creek is crying,
Maybe like me it has a grief that day and night is lasting.

Parted from the sweet loved one, candle all on your own sit,
This is the decree of heaven, whether you burn or endure it.

Go to the garden and from the bulbul all about love's mystery learn,
Come to the gathering so that from Hafiz ghazal singing you learn.

(W-C 531) The radif here translates into different terms such as "You may kindle"; "Gold-gathering"; "You stitch" & etc.

[1] "...New Year's breeze..." Noruz – the New Year marks the beginning of spring in Iran and is an important festival pre-dating historical Islam. It can last for three to six days (W-C).

[2] "...Karun..." See glossary in volume one.

[3] "...the lord of the New Year..." As one might speak of the 'spirit of Christmas'.

Ze kooye yaar miaayad nasime baade nowroozi   ز کوی یار می اید نسیم باد نوروزی
Azin baad ar madad khaahi cheraaghe del baraf roozi   ازین باد ار مدد خواهی چراغ دل برافروزی

Cho gol gar khordei daari khodaa raa sarfe eshrat kon   چو گل گر خرده ای داری خدا را صرف عشرت کن
Ke ghaaroon raa ghalat haa daad sovdaaye zar andoozi   که قارون را غلط ها داد سودای زر اندوزی

Sokhan dar parde migooyam cho gol az ghonche biroon aay   سخن در پرده می گویم چو گل از غنچه بیرون آی
Ke bish az panj roozi nist Hokme mire nowroozi   که بیش از پنج روزی نیست حکم میر نوروزی

Meyee daaram cho jaan saafiyyo soofi mikonad eybash   میی دارم چو جان صافیّ و صوفی می کند عیش
Khodaayaa hich aaghel raa mabaadaa bakhte bad roozi   خدایا هیچ عاقل را مبادا بخت بد روزی

Tarighe kaam bakhshi chist tarke kaame khod kardan   طریق کام بخشی چیست ترک کام خود کردن
Kolaahe sarvari aan ast kaz in tark bar doozi   کلاه سروری آن است کز این ترک بر دوزی

Nadaanam novheye ghomri be tarfe jooybaar az chist   ندانم نوحه قمری به طرف جویبار از چیست
Magar ou niz hamchon man ghami daarad shabaan roozi   مگر او نیز همچون من غمی دارد شبانروزی

Jodaa shod yaare shirinat konoon tanhaa neshin ey sha-m   جدا شد یار شیرینت کنون تنها نشین ای شمع
Ke hokme aasmaan in ast agar saazi vagar soozi   که حکم آسمان این است اگر سازی وگر سوزی

Be bostaan shov ke az bolbol romooze eshgh giri yaad   به بستان شو که از بلبل رموز عشق گیری یاد
Be majles aay kaz Hafez ghazal goftan biyaamoozi   به مجلس آی کز حافظ غزل گفتن بیاموزی

Of the wine of love that gives every raw one maturity,
Though it is the month of Ramadan[1] bring a cup for me.

It has been many days that have passed[2] since touched by me,
Was the leg of a tree-tall one, the forearm of one with silver body.

O heart, though like a dear guest it is, this fasting,
Its presence is a blessing, a gift also is its departing.

Just now a wise bird does not fly to the door where is preaching,
Because there is a trap wherever they gather for sermonising.

I don't complain of the puritan's bad temper, for it's like this,
When dawn breaks brightly, following hard on it the night is.

When in the garden my beloved strolls easily[3],
O breeze to that one take a message from me.

The comrade who, day and night, drinks pure wine,
Is he recalling one who drinks the dregs of wine.

If the Asaf[4] of the time doesn't do your heart justice, Hafiz,
To get what you selfishly desire by yourself a difficulty is.

(W-C 532) The radif here translates into different terms such as "A great cup"; "One silver of limb"; "A favour" & etc.

[1] "..Ramadan..." The month of fasting in Islam.

[2] "..Many days passed..." During Ramadan physical intercourse is allowed only at night, when the fasting is finished for the day, and before dawn. Since there are also additional prayers as well in the longer summer fasts marital activity is often in practise limited.

[3] "..my beloved strolls easily..." During fasting the soul is fed and has ease whilst the body struggles; here perhaps Hafiz is addressing his own soul as beloved. Thus in the next verse he asks his own soul (who is drinking pure heavenly wine) if he recalls the difficulty of his body in the physical world.

[4] "..Asaf..." See glossary in volume one.

Zaan meye eshgh kazoo pokhte shavad har khaami
Garche maahe ramezaan ast biyaavar jaami

زان می عشق کزاو پخته شود هر خامی
گرچه ماه رمضان است بیاور جامی

Rooz haa raft ke daste mane meskin nagereft
Saaghe shemshaad ghadi saaede sim andaami

روزها رفت که دست من مسکین نگرفت
ساق شمشاد قدی ساعد سیم اندامی

Rooze har chand ke mehmaane aziz ast ey del
Sohbatash movhebati daano shodan enaami

روزه هر چند که مهمان عزیز است ای دل
صحبتش موهبتی دان و شدن انعامی

Morghe zirak be dare khaane ghah aknoon naparad
Ke nahaadast be har majlese va-zi daami

مرغ زیرک به در خانقه اکنون نپرد
که نهاده ست به هر مجلس وعظی دامی

Gele az zaahede badkhoo nakonam rasm in ast
Ke cho sobhi bedamad dar peyash oftad shaami

گله از زاهد بدخو نکنم رسم این است
که چو صبحی بدمد در پی اش افتد شامی

Yaare man gar bekharaamad be tamaashaaye chaman
Beresaanash ze man ey peyke sabaa peyghaami

یار من گر بخرامد به تماشای چمن
برسانش ز من ای پیک صبا پیغامی

Aan harifi ke shabo rooz meye saaf kashad
Bovad aayaa ke konad yaad ze dord aashaami

آن حریفی که شب و روز می صاف کشد
بود آیا که کند یاد ز درد آشامی

Hafezaa gar nadahad daade delat aasafe ahd
Kaam doshvaar be dast aavari az khod kami

حافظا گر ندهد داد دلت آصف عهد
کام دشوار به دست آوری از خودکامی

At dawn a traveller within a certain territory,
To a companion repeated this riddle constantly.

O Sufi, wine gains its purity with maturity,
The number of days in the barrel must be forty[1].

If Solomon's finger is not wearing the ring[2],
What effect has the inscription of the seal ring.

A hundred-fold hatred for that robe God has,
That within its sleeve a hundred idols has.

Though generosity is a name with no trace of meaning,
Yet you tell a coquettish one[3] what it is you are needing.

O harvest owner you shall have the reward that is due,
If to one who is but a gleaner, kindness is showed by you.

Hearts are darkened; may it be that from the unseen then,
For sake of a recluse sitting in solitude, a light is given.

No hope for spiritual effort to go upward to a high region,
No cure for the heart's hurt; no suffering pain for religion.

Although being harsh is the beautiful ones' natural tendency,
How would it be if they were to tolerate one in misery.

Show me how to reach the tavern so that I can make an inquiry
From one who sees the future, as to what my final state will be.

Neither does Hafiz have presence in lessons and in seclusion's corner,
Nor is the knowledge of Certainty[4] meant for the learned scholar.

(W-C 533) The radif here translates into different terms such as "A land"; "A companion"; "A forty days space" & etc.

[1] "...forty..." Possibly a reference to the forty days of spiritual retreat called "Chilla" that was practised by Sufis.

[2] "...the ring..." Solomon's ring is associated with his power of invisible spiritual forces such as Jinns etc. The theme throughout is the importance of the inner over the outer. The ring requires that Solomon's finger is in it. The wine depends on its (inner) maturity. If inside the sleeve there is idolatry it attract God's dislike. Ask a saintly one for help even if the outer appearance shows no sign of his generosity and so on.

[3] "...coquettish..." Here it probably implies a saintly person.

[4] "...Certainty..." A level of reality witnessed by knowing mystics that goes beyond faith. It cannot be acquired by study.

Sahar gah rahrovi dar sarzamini
Hami goft in moammaa baa gharini
سحرگه رهروی در سرزمینی
همی گفت این معمّا با قرینی

Ke ey soofi sharaab aangah shaved saaf
Ke dar shishe baraarad arbaeeni
که ای صوفی شراب آنگه شود صاف
که در شیشه برآرد اربعینی

Gar angoshte soleymaani nabaashad
Che khaasiyyat dahad naghshe negini
گر انگشت سلیمانی نباشد
چه خاصیّت دهد نقش نگینی

Khodaa zaan kherghe bizaar ast sad baar
Ke sad bot baashadash dar aastini
خدا زان خرقه بیزار است صد بار
که صد بت باشدش در آستینی

Morovvat gar che naami bi neshaan ast
Niyaazi arze kon bar naazanini
مروّت گرچه نامی بی نشان است
نیازی عرضه کن بر نازنینی

Savaabat baashad ey daaraaye kharman
Agar rahmi koni bar khooshe chini
ثوابت باشد ای دارای خرمن
اگر رحمی کنی بر خوشه چینی

Daroon haa tire shod baashad ke az gheyb
Cheraaghi bar konad khalvat neshini
درونها تیره شد باشد که از غیب
چراغی برکند خلوت نشینی

Na hemmat raa omide sar bolandi
Na darmaane deli na darde dini
نه همّت را امید سربلندی
نه درمان دلی نه درد دینی

Agar che rasme khooban tond khooist
Che baashad gar besaazad baa ghamini
اگرچه رسم خوبان تندخوئیست
چه باشد گر بسازد با غمینی

Rahe meykhaane benmaa taa beporsam
Ma-aale haale khod az pish bini
ره میخانه بنما تا بپرسم
مآل حال خود از پیش بینی

Na Hafez raa hozoore darso khalvat
Na daanesh mand raa elmol yaghini
نه حافظ را حضور درس و خلوت
نه دانشمند را علم الیقینی

Since in Iraq[1] Salma has been staying,
From separation I suffer this suffering.

Driver of the camel in whose litter the friend journeys,
For riders and passenger the purpose of my longing is.

Wine drink, and throw wisdom in the Zindeh River[2],
To the sweet sound of many a young Iraqi singer.

O Saki come and a great tankard of wine bring to me,
May Allah provide for you from a bowl bountifully.

It brings my young days back into my memory,
The sound of harp and hand dancing[3] of the Saki.

Give the wine remaining, so with joyful heart, drunkenly,
The remainder of my life for friends can be given gladly.

Due to the friend's absence, blood my heart is,
May it be the hard time of separation vanishes.

In your meadow sanctuary the spring of life there is,
Allah be the shelter for the time when union there is.

Share a moment in time with those of good will to you,
The opportunity for a united gathering greatly value.

O daughter of the vine such a good bride you make,
But at times you deserve that divorce one should take.

The Messiah[4], the single one, only he,
Should have the sun for his company.

Chances for union we have let slip away;
Hafiz, Iraki ghazals speaking of separation say.

Don't disregard the tears that fall when you have departed,
From small streams like this great oceans have started.

(W-C 534) *Several of these couplets are in Arabic. Salma is the Arabic name of a beautiful woman implying the beloved.*

[1] *"..Iraq..." Western Persia rather than what we know as Iraq today.*

[2] *"..Zindeh River..."a river flowing through Isfahan.*

[3] *"..hand-waving..." This is associated with Sufis dancing in a state of ecstasy.*

[4] *"..The Messiah,...sun for company..." Jesus Christ is associated in Sufi belief with the fourth heaven – as is the sun.*

Soleimaa monzo hallat bel eraaghi
Olaaghi men navaahaa maa olaaghi

سليمى منذ حلت بالعراق
الاقى من نواها ما الاقى

Alaa ey saarebaane mahmele doost
Elaa rok baa nokom taalash tiyaaghi

الا اى ساربان محمل دوست
الى ركبانكم طال اشتياقى

Kherad dar zende rood andaazo mey nosh
Be gol baange javaanaanne eraaghi

خرد در زنده رود انداز و مى نوش
به گلبانگ جوانان عراقى

Biyaa saaghi bede ratle geraanam
Saghaakal laaho men ka-sen dehaaghi

بيا ساقى بده رطل گرانم
سقاك الله من كأس دهاق

Javaani baaz miaarad be yaadam
Samaa e chango dast afshaane saaghi

جوانى باز مى آرد به يادم
سماع چنگ و دست افشان ساقى

Meye baaghi bede taa masto khosh del
Be yaaraan bar feshaanam omre baaghi

مى باقى بده تا مست و خوشدل
به ياران برفشانم عمر باقى

Daroonam khoon shod az naadidane doost
Alaa ta-san le ayyaamel feraaghi

درونم خون شد از ناديدن دوست
الا تعسا لايّم الفراق

Rabiol omre fi mar aa hemaakom
Hamaakal laaho yaa ahdat talaaghi

ربيع العمر فى مرعى حماكم
حماك الله يا عهد التّلاقى

Dami baa nik khaahaan mottafegh baash
Ghanimat daan omoore ettefaaghi

دمى با نيك خواهان متّفق باش
غنيمت دان امور اتّفاقى

Aroosi bas khoshi ey dokhtare raz
Vali gah gah sezaavaare talaaghi

عروسى بس خوشى اى دختر رز
ولى گه گه سزاوار طلاقى

Masihaaye mojarrad raa baraazad
Ke baa khorshid saazad ham vesaaghi

مسيحاى مجرّد را برازد
كه با خورشيد سازد هم وثاقى

Mazat farsal vesaalo maa sha er naa
Begoo Hafez ghazal haaye feraaghi

مضت فرص الوصال و ما شعرنا
بگو حافظ غزلهاى فراقى

Domooee ba-dakom laa tah gheroohaa
Fakam bahren amighen men savaaghi

دموعى بعدكم لا تحقروها
فكم بحرعميق من سواقى

To the breeze at dawn I was telling my tale of longing;
Word came – "On the kindnesses of the Lord be relying."

Early morning pleading and night's sigh are key to the sought treasure,
To reach the beloved travel this way, in this style and in this manner.

The pen has not a tongue that can reveal love's mystery,
An explanation of longing is more than narrating a story[1].

Hey, Joseph of Egypt, kept so busy with administration,
Ask of the father where in the end a son's love has gone.

This wayward old world has in its nature sympathy for none,
In loving it what do you want; why give it so much attention?

How long will a high Huma bird[2] like you, find bones attractive,
It's so sad that to the unworthy your shadow's benefit you give.

If in this market there's profit it's from the contented dervish,
O God, bless me with being a contented one and a dervish.

Hafiz don't give your heart to those beauties, see the infidelities,
That the Turks of Samarqand visited on those Kharazamis[3].

To Hafiz Shirazi's ghazals, they whirl and dance, these,
Samarqandi Turks and those black-eyed Kashmiris.

(W-C 535) The radif here translates into different terms such as "Of my longing"; "Of wisdom"; "filial love" & etc.

[1] *"...than narrating a story..." Possibly a reference to Sura Yusuf in the holy Qur'an. The entire story is a narrative concerning the fulfilment of a dream of Prophet Yusuf (Joseph). In some respects it can considered to be the model for storytelling. The reference in the next verse is explicit.*

[2] *"...Huma bird..." A legendary bird that brings good fortune to all on whom its shadow falls. Avery says it was supposed not to eat flesh but only bones. Here Hafiz is probably saying that one who has a high spiritual stature should not be attracted to the world of physical forms such as physically attractive persons. This is made clear in the subsequent verses.*

[3] *"...Kharazamis..." See Avery's notes on pp 521 where he indicates a historical allusion to Tamerlane. Hafiz however finds a spiritual dimension in these historical references. In the last verse he seems to be saying these physical beauties are subordinate to the spirituality implicit in Hafiz's verses.*

Sahar baa baad migoftam hadise aarezoo mandi	سحر با باد می گفتم حدیث آرزومندی
Khetaab aamad ke vaasegh sho be altaafe khodaavandi	خطاب آمد که واثق شو به الطاف خداوندی
Doaaye sobho aahe shab kelide ganje magh sood ast	دعای صبح و آه شب کلید گنج مقصود است
Bedin raaho ravesh miro ke dar deldaar peyvandi	بدین راه و روش می رو که در دلدار پیوندی
Ghalam raa aan zabaan nabvad ke serre eshgh gooyad baaz	قلم را آن زبان نبود که سرّ عشق گوید باز
Varaaye hadde taghrir ast sharhe aarezoo mandi	ورای حدّ تقریر است شرح آرزومندی
Alaa ey yoosofe mesri ke kardat saltanat mash ghoul	الا ای یوسف مصری که کردت سلطنت مشغول
Pedar raa baaz pors aakher kojaa shod mehre farzandi	پدر را باز پرس آخر کجا شد مهر فرزندی
Jahaane pire ra-naa raa tarahhom dar jebellat nist	جهان پیر رعنا را ترّحم در جبلّت نیست
Ze eshghe ou che mijooee dar ou hemmat che mibandi	ز عشق او چه می جوئی در او همّت چه می بندی
Homaaee chon to aali ghadr herse ostokhaan heif ast	همائی چون تو عالی قدر حرص استخوان حیف است
Darigh aan saayeye hemmat ke bar naa ahl afkandi	دریغ آن سایه همّت که بر نااهل افکندی
Dar in bazaar agar soodist baa darvishe khorsand ast	درین بازار اگر سودیست با درویش خرسند است
Khodaayaa mon emam gardaan be darvishiyyo khorsandi	خدایا منعمم گردان به درویشیّ و خرسندی
Be khoobaan del madeh Hafez bebin aan bivafaaeehaa	به خوبان دل مده حافظ ببین آن بی وفائیها
Ke baa khaarazmiyaan kardand torkaane samar ghandi	که با خوارزمیان کردند ترکان سمرقندی
Be shere Hafeze shiraz miraghsando minaazand	به شعر حافظ شیراز می رقصند و می نازند
Siyah chashmaane keshmiriyyo torkaane samar ghandi	سیه چشمان کشمیریّ و ترکان سمرقندی

O Saki it is spring, cloud for shade, and the bank of a stream in flow,
I won't tell you what to do, if you are pure hearted you will know.

In this image it's not possible to get the scent of sincerity,
Wash the dirty garment of the Sufi in the wine of purity.

This world has a mean nature; don't count on its generosity;
Worldly-wise man, don't look from the mean for constancy.

Open your ear for the bulbul is calling out loudly,
Khwaja don't fall short, from the rose scent victory.

Out of gratitude for having reached another spring,
Plant the root of goodness and Reality be seeking.

You seek the beloved's face? Then make the mirror ready,
From iron[1] and brass neither rose nor jonquil grows naturally.

Two words of advice - follow them and a hundred treasures gain,
Enter by the door of being pleased, from the way of censure refrain.

You said, "From our Hafiz comes the scent of hypocrisy",
Well done to your breath, that caught the scent so quickly.

(W-C 536) The radif here translates into different terms such as "Say"; "Wash"; "Seek" & etc.
   [1] *"...iron..." Mirrors of course would be polished metal at the time of Hafiz. The mystic is advised to polish his heart in order to receive the image of the Divine.*
   In the penultimate verse here Hafiz gives advice about not being critical of others. In the final verse he demonstrates how to do this – by responding to criticism with a self effacing compliment. Thus he removes the sting from the criticism.

Saaghiyaa saayeye abrasto bahaaro labe jooy
Man nagooyam che kon ar ahle deli khod to begooy

ساقیا سایه ابر است و بهار و لب جوی
من نگویم چه کن ار اهل دلی خود تو بگوی

Booye yekrangi azin naghsh nemiaayad khiz
Dalghe aaloodeye soofi be meye naab beshooy

بوی یکرنگی ازین نقش نمی آید خیز
دلق آلوده صوفی به می ناب بشوی

Sefle ta-b ast jahaan bar karamash tekye makon
Ey jahaan dide sabaate ghadam az sefle majooy

سفله طبع است جهان بر کرمش تکیه مکن
ای جهاندیده ثبات قدم از سفله بجوی

Goosh bogshaay ke bolbol be faghaan migooyad
Khaaje taghsir mafarmaa gole tovfigh bebooy

گوش بگشای که بلبل به فغان می گوید
خواجه تقصیر مفرما گل توفیق ببوی

Shokre aan raa ke degar baaz rasidi be bahaar
Bikhe niki beneshaano rahe tahghigh bejooy

شکر آنرا که دگر باز رسیدی به بهار
بیخ نیکی بنشان و ره تحقیق بجوی

Rooye jaanaan talabi aayene raa ghaabel saaz
Zaan ke hargez golo nasrin nadamad zaahano rooy

روی جانان طلبی آینه را قابل ساز
زانکه هرگز گل و نسرین ندمد ز آهن و روی

Do nasihat konamat beshnovo sad ganj bebar
Az dare eysh dar aavo be rahe eyb mapooy

دو نصیحت کنمت بشنو و صد گنج ببر
از در عیش درآ و به ره عیب مپوی

Gofti az Hafeze maa booye riyaa miaayad
Afarin bar nafasat baad ke khosh bordi booy

گفتی از حافظ ما بوی ریا می آید
آفرین بر نفست باد که خوش بردی بوی

The peace and security of Allah, (whilst nights follow each other[1]
And second and third lute strings are in accord with each other),

Be upon the valley of the Arak tree, the resident there, and
The dwelling place on the hill beyond the dunes of sand[2].

One who prays for strangers in the world, I am[3],
Continuously ever in prayer for them I am.

O heart don't weep so, for in the chain of that one's tress,
What appears as distressing, is actually gathered-in-ness[4].

I am dying from my longing, O if only I had information,
On when the messenger had brought the news of union.

O Lord, wherever that one stops at any resting place,
Keep that one within your unending bountiful grace.

The comfort of every moment is my love for you,
My companion in every state; remembrance of you.

Your down increases your beauty by a hundred fold,
May you live to be a hundred glory-filled years old.

May the blackness in my heart until the Day of Resurrection,
Never be empty of feeling for you with longing and passion.

To that Powerful Designer very well done I say,
Drawing a crescent[5] on the moon's face that way.

With such a king as you how should there be union,
With a rend like me, careless and of bad reputation.

That you exist is the only absolute necessity,
Or there is only loss of capital and interest for me[6].

God knows all about Hafiz's true intent,
God's Knowledge for me is sufficient.

(W-C 537) *Some couplets are in Arabic in the original.*
[1] *"...whilst nights follow..." According to W-C this refers to reading the holy Qur'an. Often a second or third person may be checking on the accuracy of the reading by a hafiz – one who recites from memory.*
[2] *This according to Avery reflects the convention of referring to the place vacated by the beloved in Arabic love poetry.*
[3] *"...strangers in the world..." This may refer to spiritual travellers who are not at home in this world (dunya).*

Salamollaahe maa karral layaali
Va jaa vabtel masaani val masaali

سلام الله ما کرّ اللّیالی
و جاوبت المثانی و المثالی

Alaa vaadel araak va man alayhaa
Va daaren bellevaa favghal remaali

علی وادی الاراک و من علیها
و دار باللّوی فوق الرمال

Doaa gooye gharibaane jahaanam
Va ad ou bet tavaator vat tavaali

دعاگوی غریبان جهانم
و ادعو بالتّواتر و التّوالی

Manaal ey del ke dar zanjire zolfash
Hame jam iyyat ast aashofte haali

منال ای دل که در زنجیر زلفش
همه جمعیّت است آشفته حالی

Amooto sabbaton yaa layta sheri
Mataa natghal bashiro an vesaali

اموت صبابه یا لیت شعری
متی نطق البشیر عن الوصال

Be har manzel ke rooy aarad khodaayaa
Negah daarash be fazle laa yazaali

به هر منزل که روی آرد خدایا
نگه دارش به فضل لایزالی

Fahobbok raahati fi kolle hini
Va zekrok moonesi fi kolle haali

فحبّک راحتی فی کل حین
و ذکرک مونسی فی کل حال

Ze khattat sad jamaale digar afzood
Ke omrat baad sad saale jalaali

ز خطّت صد جمال دیگر افزود
که عمرت باد صد سال جلالی

Soveydaaye dele man taa ghiyaamat
Mabaad az shovgho sovdaaye to khaali

سویدای دل من تا قیامت
مباد از شوق سودای تو خالی

Bar aan nagh ghaashe ghodrat aafarin baad
Ke gerde mah kashad khatte helaali

برآن نقّاش قدرت آفرین باد
که گرد مه کشد خطّ هلالی

Kojaa yaabam vesaale chon to shaahi
Mane bad naame rende laaobaali

کجا یابم وصال چون تو شاهی
من بدنام رند لاابالی

To mibaayad ke bashi var na sahl ast
Ziyaane maayeye jahiyyo maali

تو می باید که باشی ورنه سهل است
زیان مایه جاهیّ و مالی

Khodaa vaaghef ke Hafez raa gharaz chist
Va elmollaahe hasbi men soaali

خدا واقف که حافظ را غرض چیست
و علم الله حسبی من سؤالی

---

4 "... gathered-in-ness..." Sufis practise a form of meditation or fikr which involves the heart being 'gathered in',
sometimes called "collectedness". In this the focus is on unity and the diversity of ephemeral experience is
drawn in to this..

5 "... drawing a crescent..." This could relate to the earlier verse and mean the 'down' newly formed on a
youths face.

6 "...capital and interest..." Capital being life and interest being that spiritual benefit which one earns with one's
life. Saberi translates this verse as:- "It is essential that you live/the loss of luxury and property is not important".

Salaam[1], like the fine fragrance of friendship, be,
To the pupil of an eye filled with luminosity.

Greetings, like the light in the heart of world renouncing ones,
To that candle of the corner where sit the reclusive ones.

None of the companions in their usual place do I see,
My heart is bloody with grief. Where are you O Saki?

From the street of the Magian[2] do not turn away your face,
The key to the solution of difficulties is sold in that place.

The wine that obliterates the Sufi can be bought where?
At the hand of austere hypocritical piety, torment I suffer.

Friends have broken the bonds of concord so completely,
One could say of friendships, that there had never been any.

Though the bride of the world can be attractive,
In practising infidelity she is excessively active.

If my broken heart has retained enduring constancy,
It will not seek balm from those whose hearts are stony.

O greedy carnal nature, if you were to go from me,
A sovereign's power I would get from beggary.

To gain felicity I will teach you the alchemy,
Stay away, stay away, from evil company.

Hafiz, do not make outcry against time's revolutions,
What, O slave, do you know about God's intentions.

(W-C 538)
[1] *"..Salaam..." Translated usually as peace but carrying the implication of security too. It is the traditional Muslim greeting.*
[2] *"..Magian..." See glossary in volume one.*

Salaami cho booye khoshe aash naaee
Bar aan mardome dideye rov shanaaee

سلامی چو بوی خوش آشنایی
برآن مردم دیده روشنایی

Doroodi cho noore dele paar saayaan
Bedaan sha-me khalvatgahe paar saaee

درودی چو نور دل پارسایان
بدان شمع خلوتگه پارسایی

Nemibinam az hamdamaan hich bar jay
Delam khoon shod az ghosse saaghi kojaaee

نمی بینم از همدمان هیچ بر جای
دلم خون شد از غصّه ساقی کجایی

Ze kooye moghaan rokh magardaan ke aanjaa
Forooshand meftaahe moshkel goshaaee

ز کوی مغان رخ مگردان که آنجا
فروشند مفتاح مشکل گشایی

Meye soofi afkan kojaa miforooshand
Ke dar taabam az daste zohde riyaaee

می صوفی افکن کجا می فروشند
که در تابم از دست زهد ریایی

Rafighaan chonaan ahde sohbat shekastand
Ke gooee naboodast khod aash naaee

رفیقان چنان عهد صحبت شکستند
که گویی نبودست خود آشنایی

Aroose jahaane gar che dar hadde hosn ast
Ze had mibarad shiveye bi vafaaee

عروس جهان گرچه در حدّ حسن است
ز حد می برد شیوه بی وفایی

Dele khasteye man garash hemmati hast
Nakhaahad ze sangin delaan moomiyaaee

دل خسته من گرش همّتی هست
نخواهد ز سنگین دلان مومیایی

Maraa gar to bogzaari ey nafse tame
Basi paad shaahi konam dar gedaaee

مراگر تو بگذاری ای نفس طامع
بسی پادشاهی کنم در گدایی

Biyaamoozamat kimiyaaye sa aadat
Ze ham sohbate bad jodaaee jodaaee

بیاموزمت کیمیای سعادت
ز هم صحبت بد جدایی جدایی

Makon Hafez az jovre dovraan shekaayat
Che daani to ey bande kaare khodaaee

مکن حافظ از جور دوران شکایت
چه دانی تو ای بنده کار خدایی

At dawn, the tavern's messenger, unseen, wishing me well,
Said, "Return, in this place as a regular you're known well.

Like Jamshid take our wine so that the two world's mystery
In the ray of light from that world revealing cup, you may see.

At the tavern door are the Rends who wander free,
Who give or take at will the crown of sovereignty.

Their head on a brick[1], but underfoot are the 'seven sisters'[2],
See the power wielding hand and the dignity of its officers.

Our head unites with the doorstep of the tavern, whose ceiling,
Despite the lowness of its walls, up to the heavens is reaching.

Do not try for this stage, without Khizr[3] accompanying,
In such darkness be very wary of the danger of straying.

O heart, if on you is bestowed the kingdom of poverty,
Your smallest domain from the moon to the fish[4] will be.

Can't breathe the air of poverty? Then don't lose your grip,
On the concourse of Turanshah[5] and the platform of lordship.

O crude and greedy Hafiz, be very ashamed of what you say,
What work did you do that the two worlds you desire for pay.

(W-C 539)
[1] "...head on a brick..." Using a brick as a pillow.
[2] "...seven-sisters..." The Pleiades star formation.
[3] "...Khizr..." See glossary in volume one.
[4] "...the moon to the fish..." From the heights to the depths.
[5] "...Turanshah..." The chief minister of Shah Shuja.

Saharam haatafe mey khaane be dovlat khaahi

سحرم هاتف میخانه به دولت خواهی

Goft baaz aay ke dirineye in dargaahi

گفت بازآی که دیرینه این درگاهی

Hamcho jam jor eye maa kash ke ze serre do jahaan

همچو جم جرعه ما کش که ز سرّ دو جهان

Partove jaame jahaan bin dahadat aagaahi

پرتو جام جهان بین دهدت آگاهی

Bar dare meykade rendaane ghalandar baashand

بر در میکده رندان قلندر باشند

Ke setaanando dahand afsare shaahan shaahi

که ستانند و دهند افسر شاهنشاهی

Khesht zire saro bar taaraake haft akhtar pay

خشت زیر سر و بر تارک هفت اختر پای

Daste ghodrat negaro mansabe saaheb jaahi

دست قدرت نگر و منصب صاحب جاهی

Sare maavo dar meykhaane ke tarfe baamash

سر ما و در میخانه که طرف بامش

Be falak bar shodo divaar bedin kootaahi

به فلک بر شد و دیوار بدین کوتاهی

Ghat e in marhale bi hamrahiye khezr makon

قطع این مرحله بی همرهی خضر مکن

Zolomaatast betars az khatare gomraahi

ظلمات است بترس از خطر گمراهی

Agarat saltanate faghr bebakhshand ey del

اگرت سلطنت فقر ببخشند ای دل

Kamtarin molke to az maah bovad taa maahi

کمترین ملک تو از ماه بود تا ماهی

To dame faghr nadaani zadan az dast madeh

تو دم فقر ندانی زدن از دست مده

Masnade khaajegiyo majlese tooraan shaahi

مسند خواجگی و مجلس توران شاهی

Hafeze khaam tama sharmi azin ghesse badaar

حافظ خام طمع شرمی ازین قصّه بدار

Amalat chist ke mozdash do jahaan mikhaahi

عملت چیست که مزدش دو جهان می خواهی

The heart is full of pain! No salve there is! Oh dear!
Lord, a friend, or my heart will die of loneliness, I fear.

Who looks to the changing heavens for comfort and ease?
O Saki, so that I may get some respite bring a cup please.

Get up, so to the Samarkandi saucepot our heart we may be giving,
For from that breeze, the scent of Mulian's stream is ever coming[1].

I said to a witty one, "Just look at these states!" Laughing, he said,
"Difficult work O Father of wonders! The world is turned on its head!"

For the candle of Chigil[2] in the well of patience I was burning
Where is a Rustam?[3] Our state the Turkish king is not heeding.

In the Way of love-play, ease and safety are a calamity,
May that heart be wounded that for its pain seeks remedy.

To the street of Rends the indulgent and self-satisfing can't go,
It needs a world-burning traveller, not one raw with no sorrow.

From this world of dust to hand comes no proper man,
It is necessary to make another world and a new man[4].

Hafiz when love has no need what good will your crying do,
For in this great deluge the seven seas are merely a drop of dew.

(W-C 540) The radif here translates into different terms such as "A plaster"; "A companion"; "A while"
& etc.

[1] *"...According to Avery a reference to an episode in which the ruler's subjects wished to inspire him to return to their homelands, A poet was asked to write a verse that would bring this desire on him. It was successful. See Avery's more comprehensive note on pp.557.*

[2] *"...Chigil..." This is a city known for its beautiful women.*

[3] *"...Rustam..." This is a legendary warrior known for his strength.*

[4] *"...a new man..." Conceivably this is a reference to a Qur'an passage in which Allah says "He can make another people to succeed you". Sura Hud. Verse 57.*

Sine maalaamaale dard ast ey darighaa marhami
Del ze tanhaaee be jaan aamad khodaa raa hamdami

سینه مالامال درد است ای دریغا مرهمی
دل ز تنهائی به جان آمد خدارا همدمی

Chashme aasaayesh ke daarad az sepehre tiz rov
Saaghiyaa jaami be man deh taa biyaasaayam dami

چشم آسایش که دارد از سپهر تیز رو
ساقیا جامی به من ده تا بیاسایم دمی

Khiz taa khaater badaan torke samarghandi dahim
Kaz nasimash booye jooye mooliyaan aayad hami

خیز تا خاطر بدان ترک سمرقندی دهیم
کز نسیمش بوی جوی مولیان آید همی

Ziraki raa goftam in ahvaal bin khandido goft
Sa-b roozi bolajab kaari parishaan aalami

زیرکی را گفتم این احوال بین خندید و گفت
صعب روزی بوالعجب کاری پریشان عالمی

Sookhtam dar chaahe sabr az bahre aan sham-e chegel
Shaahe torkaan faaregh ast az haale maa koo rostami

سوختم در چاه صبر از بهر آن شمع چگل
شاه ترکان فارغ است از حال ما کو رستمی

Dar tarighe eshgh baazi amno aasaayesh balaast
Rish baad aan del ke baa dared to khaahad marhami

در طریق عشقبازی امن و آسایش بلاست
ریش باد آن دل که با درد تو خواهد مرهمی

Ahle kaamo naaz raa dar kooye rendi raah nist
Rahrovi baayad jahaan soozi na khaami bi ghami

اهل کام و ناز را در کوی رندی راه نیست
رهروی باید جهان سوزی نه خامی بیغمی

Aadami dar aalame khaki nemiaayad be dast
Aalami digar bebaayad saakht vaz nov aadami

آدمی در عالم خاکی نمی آید به دست
عالمی دیگر بباید ساخت وز نو آدمی

Geryeye Hafez che sanjad pishe estegh naaye eshgh
Kandarin toofaan nomaayad haft daryaa shabnami

گریه حافظ چه سنجد پیش استغنای عشق
کاندرین طوفان نماید هفت دریا شبنمی

Come Saki, with wine the tulip cup has become filled up,
How long to mutter nonsense and mumbo-jumbo make up.

Pride and arrogance leave, for witness time is bearing,
To Caesar's robe crumpling and Kay's[1] crown crumbling.

Become aware! For intoxicated the meadow's bird has become;
Wake up, watch out! The sleep of oblivion upon you will come.

How graciously you sway, fresh branch of spring,
May winter's first winds no distress to you bring.

There is no trusting the vagaries of the sphere's liking,
That's bad for one who feels secure from its deceiving.

Tomorrow for us wine of the eternal fountain and the Houri there is,
Today too the moon faced Saki and the cup of wine there is.

The dawn breeze brings memories of childhood our way,
O young boy bring the medicine that takes sorrow away.

The grandeur and lordship of the rose don't regard; the reason is,
The wind will sweep away each petal till a carpet underfoot it is.

Bring the huge jug of wine in Hatim Tai's[2] memory,
So we can wrap up the black record of the miserly.

From the wine that gives beauty and softness to the Judas tree,
To its face and delicate disposition sweat comes naturally.

Carry the throne to the garden because just as servants do,
The Cypress stands to attend; the Ney's[3] loins are girded up too.

Hafiz the story of your magical deceptive words travelled far,
All the way to Rum, Rey, and the borders of Egypt and China.

(W-C 541) This ghazal is described by W-C as a true example of the Shirazi dialect.
  [1] *"...Kay's..." Kay was a famous king of 5th century BC.*
  [2] *"...Hatim Tai..." A fabulously wealthy and generous man.*
  [3] *"...Ney's..." The ney is a reed pipe made famous by the first lines of the Masnevi of Maulana Rumi.*

Saaghi biyaa ke shod ghadahe laale por ze mey
Taamaat taa be chando khoraafaat taa be key

ساقی بیا که شد قدح لاله پر ز می
طامات تا به چند و خرافات تا به کی

Bogzar ze kebro naaz ke didast roozegaar
Chine ghabaaye gheysaro tarfe kolaahe key

بگذر ز کبر و ناز که دیده ست روزگار
چین قبای قیصر و طرف کلاه کی

Hoshyaar shov ke morghe chaman mast gasht haan
Bidaar shov ke khaabe adam dar pey ast hey

هشیّار شو که مرغ چمن مست گشت هان
بیدار شو که خواب عدم در پی است هی

Khosh naazokaane michami ey shaakhe novbahaar
Kaashoftegi mabaadat az aashoobe baade dey

خوش نازکانه می چمی ای شاخ نوبهار
کاشفتگی مبادت از آشوب باد دی

Bar mehre charkho shiveye ou e-temaad nist
Ey vaay bar kasi ke shod imen ze makre vey

بر مهر چرخ و شیوه او اعتماد نیست
ای وای بر کسی که شد ایمن ز مکر وی

Fardaa sharaabe kowsaro hoor az baraaye mast
Vem rooz niz saaghiye mahrooyo jaame mey

فردا شراب کوثر و حور از برای ماست
و امروز نیز ساقی مهروی و جام می

Baade sabaa ze ahde sebi yaad midahad
Jaan daarooee ke gham bebarad dar deh ey sobey

باد صبا ز عهد صبی یاد می دهد
جان داروئی که غم ببرد در ده ای صبیّ

Heshmat mabino saltanate gol ke besporad
Farraashe baad har varaghash raa be zire pey

حشمت مبین و سلطنت گل که بسپرد
فرّاش باد هر ورقش را به زیر پی

Dar deh be yaade haatame tey jaame yek mani
Taa naameye siyaahe bakhilaan konim tey

در ده به یاد حاتم طی جام یک منی
تا نامه سیاه بخیلان کنیم طی

Zaan mey ke daad hosno letaafat be arghavaan
Biroon fekand lotfe mezaaj az rokhash be khey

زان می که داد حسن و لطافت به ارغوان
بیرون فکند لطف مزاج از رخش به خوی

Masnad be baagh bar ke be khedmat cho bandegaan
Estaade ast sarvo kamar baste ast ney

مسند به باغ بر که به خدمت چو بندگان
استاده است سرو و کمر بسته است نی

Hafez hadise sehr faribe khoshat rasid
Taa hadde mesro chino be atraafe roomo rey

حافظ حدیث سحر فریب خوشت رسید
تا حدّ مصر و چین و به اطراف روم و ری

It is a city full of slender ones[1] – on every side another beauty,
It is an invitation to love, if to undertake work you are ready

The eye of the world won't see a youth fresher than this,
Into no one's hand falls a lovelier beloved one than this.

A body created from a soul, whoever saw such thing?
Let no dust from the clay-bound that one's dress be soiling.

Why do you drive away a broken one like me,
When all I seek is a kiss, or an embrace maybe?

The wine is pure! Quick, the time is right, use it well,
Who has the hope of such a spring next year as well?

In the garden, the tulip and the rose keep company,
To the beloved's face each raises a cup in memory.

How to loosen this knot or expose this wound's mystery?
A pain, a severe pain?[2] Work! Work of great difficulty.

Every hair of Hafiz is held by a carefree beauty,
To stay in this country is difficult of a certainty.

(W-C 542) The radif here translates into different terms such as "An idol"; "A bargain"; "A particle of dust" & etc.

[1] "...a city full of slender ones..." Here conceivably Hafiz speaks of a city in the Unseen where the souls dwell in unalloyed beauty; or possibly he refers to the Houris who cannot be seen by the eyes made of clay. Perhaps in verse four he refers to difficulty in getting access to that spiritual domain and in the last verse refers to the difficulty of staying there.

[2] "...It's a pain..." There is a well known saying that paradise is surrounded by things we do not like. Enduring much pain, Hafiz may be suggesting, is a route to this city of beauties.

Shahrist por zarifaan vaz har taraf negaari

Yaaraan salaaye eshgh ast gar mikonid kaari

شهریست پر ظریفان وز هر طرف نگاری
یاران صلای عشق است گر می کنید کاری

Chashme jahaan nabinad zin taaze tar javaani

Dar daste kas nayoftad zin khoob tar negaari

چشم جهان نبیند زین تازه تر جوانی
در دست کس نیفتد زین خوبتر نگاری

Jesmi ke dide baashad kaz roohash aafaridand

Zin khaakiyaan mabaadaa bar daamanash ghobaari

جسمی که دیده باشد کز روحش آفریدند
زین خاکیان مبادا بر دامنش غباری

Chon man shekastei raa az pishe khod che raani

Kam ghaayate tavagh gho boosist yaa kenaari

چون من شکسته ای را از پیش خود چه رانی
کم غایت توقّع بوسیست یا کناری

Mey bi ghash ast beshtaab vaghti khosh ast daryaab

Saale degar ke daarad ommide nov bahaari

می بیغش است بشتاب وقتی خوش است دریاب
سال دگر که دارد امّید نوبهاری

Dar boostaan harifaan maanande laalevo gol

Har yek gerefte jaami bar yaade rooye yaari

در بوستان حریفان مانند لاله و گل
هر یک گرفته جامی بر یاد روی یاری

Chon in gereh goshaayam vin rish chon nomaayam

Dardiyo sa-b dardi kaariyyo sakht kaari

چون این گره گشایم وین ریش چون نمایم
دردی و صعب دردی کاری و سخت کاری

Har tare mooye Hafez dar daste zolf shookhist

Moshkel tavaan neshastan dar in diyaar baari

هر تاره موی حافظ در دست زلف شوخیست
مشکل توان نشستن در این دیار باری

On love's existence dependent are Man and Peri,
Demonstrate desire so you may find a fine felicity.

Since you don't have inner sight, don't look for union,
The cup of Jamshid[1] is of no use to one without vision.

O venerable elder, strive so that lacking love you are not,
For no one purchases a slave who no skill has got.

How long the sweet sleep[2] and the wine of the morning?
Strive, with pleading at midnight and with dawn weeping.

Come; buy from us sovereignty with the cash of beauty,
Do not be careless in this trade or regretful you will be.

Supplication by the secluded corner-sitter averts disaster,
So why not look towards us out of your eye's corner.

How can I remedy my amazement at both union and separation?
You are neither before the eye nor absent from perception[3].

A thousand holy souls were consumed by the fire of envy,
That each dawn you are the candle of a different assembly.

Since a doorway to bewilderment was found in every piece of news,
In future intoxication and I will be one with the state of hearing no news.

Come, because the state of the world I have looked at fully,
You will drink wine not sorrow if you examine it similarly.

From the blessing on Hafiz's spiritual striving, an omen I am taking,
That in the moonlight on the path, the sign of Laila[4] I'll be finding[5].

Who will deliver to his highness Asaf[6] a message from me,
Saying commit two verses of mine in old Dari[7] to memory?

May the royal crown not slide down on the head of your beauty!
You deserve both throne and gold crown for you are fortune's beauty.

To get what they need from your hair and face they come and go daily,
The dawn breeze for musk to distribute, the rose to gather its beauty.

(W-C 544)
[1] *"...the cup of Jamshid..." In which one can see various levels of the divine reality. Hafiz seems to be saying that to reach to a stage of union with the Beloved (God) this is necessary to have. You can however still know the bliss of love.*
[2] *"...How long the sweet sleep..." The dawn prayers for Muslims are short and because of the early hour it is tempting afterwards to sleep. Khwaja Muinuddin Hasan Chishti in, however, says that one who remains on the prayer carpet after the prayer and is engaged in remembrance get the reward of admission to heaven – along with seventy associates. (See the Meditations of Khwaja Muinuddin Hasan Chishti; Sharib Press).*
[3] *"...You are neither before the eye nor absent from perception..." Only the mystic who has known union can*

Tofeyle hastiye eshghand adamiyyo pari Eraadati benomaa taa sa-aadati bebari	طفیل هستی عشقند آدمیّ و پری ارادتی بنما تا سعادتی ببری
Cho mostaedde nazar nisti vesaal majooy Ke jaame jam nakonad sood vaghte bi basari	چو مستعدّ نظر نیستی وصال مجوی که جام جم نکند سود وقت بی بصری
Bekoosh khaajevo az eshgh bi nasib mabaash Ke bande raa nakharad kas be eybe bi honari	بکوش خواجه و از عشق بی نصیب مباش که بنده را نخرد کس به عیب بی هنری
Meye sabooho shekar khaabe sobh dam taa chand Be ozre nim shabi koosho geryeye sahari	می صبوح و شکر خواب صبحدم تا چند به عذر نیم شبی کوش و گریه سحری
Biyaavo saltanat az maa bekhar be maayeye hosn Vazin moaamele ghaafel mashov ke heyf khori	بیا و سلطنت از ما بخر به مایه حسن وزین معامله غافل مشو که حیف خوری
Doaaye gooshe neshinaan balaa begardaanad Cheraa be goosheye chashmi be maa neminegari	دعای گوشه نشینان بلا بگرداند چرا به گوشه چشمی به ما نمی نگری
Ze hejro vasle to dar heyratam che chaare konam Na dar baraabare chashmi na ghaayeb az nazari	زهجر و وصل تو در حیرتم چه چاره کنم نه در برابر چشمی نه غایب از نظری
Hezaar jaane moghaddas besookht zin gheyrat Ke har sabaaho masaa sha-me majlese degari	هزار جان مقدّس بسوخت زین غیرت که هر صباح و مسا شمع مجلس دگری
Cho har khabar ke shanidam dari be heyrat daasht Azin sepas mano mastiyyo vaz-e bi khabari	چو هر خبر که شنیدم دری به حیرت داشت ازین سپس من و مستی و وضع بی خبری
Biyaa ke vaz-e jahaan raa chonaan ke man didam Gar emtehaan bekoni mey khoriyyo gham nakhori	بیا که وضع جهان را چنانکه من دیدم گر امتحان بکنی می خوری و غم نخوری
Be yomne hemmate Hafez omid hast ke baaz Araa osaamero leylaaye laylatol ghamari	به یمن همّت حافظ امید هست که باز اری اسامر لیلای لیله القمری
Ze man be Hazrate aasef ke mibarad peyghaam Ke yaad gir do mesra ze man be nazme dari	ز من به حضرت آصف که می برد پیغام که یادگیر دو مصرع ز من به نظم دری
Kolaahe sarvariyat kaj mabaad bar sare hosn Ke zibe bakhto sezaavaare molko taaje sari	کلاه سروریت کج مباد بر سر حسن که زیب بخت و سزاوار ملک و تاج سری
Be booye zolfo rokhat miravando miaayand Sabaa be ghaaliye saaeeyyo gol be jelvegari	به بوی زلف و رخت می روند و می آیند صبا به غالیه سائی و گل به جلوه گری

really understand the brilliance of this description of union, and of separation.

4 "...Laila..." The beloved of Majnun. See glossary in volume one.

5 This line is Arabic in the original. It would seem here Hafiz maybe saying that he has seen in vision, derived from his spiritual striving, that he will find again, in the light of the holy Prophet, the reality of 'There is no God but God'. The holy Prophet is often identified with the moon symbolically. Laila refers to the Beloved (God), but, based on the sounds in the word, may imply the Muslim article of faith.

6 "...Asaf..." See glossary in volume one.

7 "...Dari..." An ancient Persian language.

Everything that you desire in the world you have,
But grief for the weak and powerless do you have?

Ask heart and life from your slave; and take the soul,
For over the free ones the right of command you have.

You have no middle[1] so it's surprising that all the time,
In the circle of beauties the middle place you have.

No painting can show off the whiteness of your face better than,
The musky, fine, black, downy line[2] on arghavan[3] you already have.

Light of soul and delicate you are so drink wine always,
Especially at this time when a heavy head you have.

Don't show more anger and injustice to our heart than this,
When it is possible, do what you like; this choice you have.

If a hundred thousand arrows of tyranny you may possess,
The intent to aim them at my wounded life's blood you have.

Endure happily the guardian's injustice and harsh jealousy,
It is easy enough if the kindness of the friend you have.

If, for one breath, union with the friend you take hold of,
Go, for every desirable thing in the world, you have.

Hafiz, when you are carrying of a rose from the garden bed,
What care for the gardener's moans and groans should you have?

(W-C 545) See appendix; (W-C 546) See appendix; (W-C 547) See appendix; (W-C 548) See appendix
(W-C 549) See appendix; (W-C 550) See appendix
(W-C 551) The radif here, which we have used, is "You have".
  [1] "...have no middle..." Has also been translated as waist or centre. The slender waist is an often used image
  for the beloved. It is also an image for the link between man and God (Isthmus). Perhaps, also, one may say
  that infinity can have no centre.
  [2] "...black downy line..." This can refer to the down on a young man's face before it becomes a beard. The
  significant thing is that it emphasis youthfulness. It could however also refer to the down on a female face

Toraa ke harche moraad ast dar jahaan daari

Che gham ze haale zaeefaane naatavaan daari

ترا که هرچه مراد است در جهان داری

چه غم ز حال ضعیفان ناتوان داری

Bekhaah jaano del az bandevo ravaan bestaan

Ke hokm bar sare aazaadegaan ravaan daari

بخواه جان و دل از بنده و روان بستان

که حکم بر سر آزادگان روان داری

Miyaan nadaariyo daaram ajab ke har saa-at

Miyaane majmae khoobaan koni miyaan daari

میان نداری و دارم عجب که هر ساعت

میان مجمع خوبان کنی میان داری

Bayaaze rooye to raa nist naghsh dar khor azaank

Savaadi az khate moshkin bar arghavaan daari

بیاض روی ترا نیست نقش درخور ازآنک

سوادی از خط مشکین بر ارغوان داری

Benoosh mey ke sabok roohiyo latif modaam

Alal khosoos dar in dam ke sar geraan daari

بنوش می که سبک روحی و لطیف مدام

علی الخصوص دراین دم که سر گران داری

Makon etaab azin bisho jovr bar dele maa

Bekon har aanche tavaani ke jaaye aan daari

مکن عتاب ازین بیش و جور بر دل ما

بکن هرآنچه توانی که جای آن داری

Be ekhtiyaarat agar sad hezaar tire jafaast

Be ghasde khoone mane khaste dar kamaan daari

به اختیارت اگر صد هزار تیر جفاست

به قصد خون من خسته در کمان داری

Bekash jafaaye raghibaan modaamo jovre hasood

Ke sahl baashad agar yaare mehrabaan daari

بکش جفای رقیبان مدام و جور حسود

که سهل باشد اگر یار مهربان داری

Be vasle doost garat dast midahad yek dam

Boro ke har che moraad ast dar jahaan daari

به وصل دوست گرت دست می دهد یکدم

برو که هر چه مراد است در جهان داری

Cho gol be daaman azin baagh mibari Hafez

Che gham ze naalevo faryaade baaghbaan daari

چو گل به دامن ازین باغ می بری حافظ

چه غم ز ناله و فریاد باغبان داری

that enhances the faces beauty. Miniature pictures often show female and male faces with a darkened line around the edge. Mystically 'down' can imply a line from the Qur'an or the perception of fine detail in phenomena.

[3] "...arghavan's hue..." A light pink/purplish colour associated with the flower. See https://www.flickr.com/photos/ye_doost/3387490291

If, in the rose-garden, like a tall cypress you were to be sauntering,
From envy of your face every rose would feel the thorn's sting.

From the infidelity of your hair's curls, every circle is in confusion
From the magic in your eye's look, every corner has a sick person.

O drunken eye of the beloved do not, like my luck, be sleeping,
For from every quarter the sigh of an awakening one is arriving.

The scattering of your path's dust is my very life's currency,
Even though in the life of the soul no value you deign to see.

Heart; don't go on about the heart-catching hair of the dear ones.
How can your work be successful when thoughts are dark ones?

My head carried on, so not for a moment did work continue,
My heart was constricted, but no care for a captive have you.

I told that one to be in my circle like the centre point of a compass
Laughing, that one said, "O Hafiz, which particular compass?"

(W-C 552) The radif here translates into different terms such as "A rose garden,"; "A thorn"; "A sick
   one" & etc.
(W-C 553) See appendix
(W-C 554) See appendix
(W-C 555) See appendix
(W-C 556) See appendix

Cho sarv agar bekharaami dami be golzaari
Khorad ze gheyrate rooye to har goli khaari

چو سرو اگر بخرامی دمی به گلزاری
خورد ز غیرت روی تو هر گلی خاری

Ze kofre zolfe to har halgheiyyo aashoobi
Ze sehre chashme to har goosheiyyo bimaari

ز کفر زلف تو هر حلقه ای و آشوبی
ز سحر چشم تو هر گوشه ای و بیماری

Marov cho bakhte man ey chashme maste yaar be khaab
Ke dar pey ast ze har sooyat aahe bidaari

مرو چو بخت من ای چشم مست یار به خواب
که در پی است ز هر سویت آه بیداری

Nesaare khaake rahat naghde jaane man har chand
Ke nist naghde ravaan raa bare to meghdaari

نثار خاک رهت نقد جان من هر چند
که نیست نقد روان را بر تو مقداری

Delaa hamishe mazan raahe zolfe delbandaan
Cho tire raay shodi key goshaayadat kaari

دلا همیشه مزن راه زلف دلبندان
چو تیره رای شدی کی گشایدت کاری

Saram berafto zamaani besar naraft in kaar
Delam gerefto naboodat dele gereftaari

سرم برفت و زمانی بسر نرفت این کار
دلم گرفت و نبودت دل گرفتاری

Cho noghte goftamash andar miyaane daayere aay
Be khande goft ke ey Hafez in che pargaari

چو نقطه گفتمش اندر میان دایره آی
به خنده گفت که ای حافظ این چه پرگاری

It is morning and hail falls from the wintery cloud of January,
Make ready the morning cup, and a large one let it be.

Into the sea of ego and self praise I have fallen, so,
Bring wine, to free me from self-praise and my ego.

The blood of the cup drink, for this blood is lawful for you,
In the work of wine-drinking be busy, it is good work to do.

Saki, be close at hand because sorrow waits to ambush us,
Maestro, this melody you're playing, keep on with it, for us.

Give wine, since the harp bent down and said very quietly,
"Listen to what this bowed wise elder says, and be happy".

Saki, give wine I say, for the sake of the Rends who have no need,
So you can hear in the song of the singer about He Who has no Need[1].

(W-C 557)

[1] *"...He Who has no Need..." This refers to God of course, Who alone has no need. The reference to 'the 'dissolute' mystics, (Rends) having no needs therefore implies they have united with God.*

Sobhasto zhaale michekad az abre bahmani

Barge sabooh saazo bedeh jaame yek mani
صبح است و ژاله می چکد از ابر بهمنی

برگ صبوح ساز و بده جام یک منی

Dar bahre maaeeyo mani oftaadeam biyaar

Mey taa khalaas bakh shadam az maaeeyo mani
در بحر مائی و منی افتاده ام بیار

می تا خلاص بخشدم از مائی و منی

Khoone piyaale khor ke halaal ast khoone ou

Dar kaare baade baash ke kaarist kardani
خون پیاله خور که حلال است خون او

در کار باده باش که کاری ست کردنی

Saaghi be dast baash ke gham dark kamine maast

Motreb negaah daar hamin rah ke mizani
ساقی به دست باش که غم در کمین ماست

مطرب نگاه دار همین ره که می زنی

Mey deh ke sar be gooshe man aavar chango goft

Khosh bogzaraano beshno azin pire monhani
می ده که سر به گوش من آورد چنگ و گفت

خوش بگذران و بشنو ازین پیر منحنی

Saaghi be bi niyaaziye rendaan ke mey bedeh

Taa beshnavi ze sovte moghanni hoval ghani
ساقی به بی نیازی رندان که می بده

تا بشنوی ز صوت مغنّی هو الغنی

Life has passed me by in lust and no fruit at all is it bearing.
So that to a good age you reach, boy, to me the wine cup bring.

In this city such sweet ones have found satisfaction,
Falcons of the Path[1], contented with the fly's situation.

With a blood filled heart, like the musk pod, that one should be happy,
Who gains universal approbation because their speaking is musky.

Spread your wings and sing out from the heavenly Tuba tree[2],
It would be a pity if a bird of your ilk should be in captivity.

The caravan gone! You asleep, on the road where ambush is waiting!
Oh dear! You are not aware of the sound of so much bell ringing[3].

"From Mount Sinai[4] I saw that a light was flashing,
To it I go and maybe for you some fire can bring."

In order to catch the beloved's garment, as with incense in a burner,
We have placed our life into the fire, so that we can get a nice odour.

How long searching every corner for you should Hafiz be,
O desirable one! May Allah make the finding of you easy.

(W-C 558)

[1] "...the Path..." This refers to the mystics who travel on the path of Tariqat. They are in search of the essence; the spirit rather than the letter of the law. As Hafiz himself says elsewhere, their creed is – "Whatever comes my way is best". "This city" may refer to Shiraz or to a city in the Unseen world.

[2] "...Tuba tree..." See glossary in volume one.

[3] "...bell-ringing..." The bells used to be rung to announce the departure of the caravan. Here he would seem to be saying - wake up spiritually!

[4] "...From Mount Sinai..." This verse is in Arabic. It is from a verse in the holy Qur'an in which Prophet Moses is attracted to Mount Sinai to get fire for his family. There he discovers the burning bush and talks to God.

It is possible to read this ghazal as describing the path from Tariqat (The Way) to Haqiqat – the Truth.

Omr bogzasht be bi haaseliyo bol havasi
Ey pesar jaame meyam deh ke be piri berasi

عمر بگذشت به بیحاصلیو و بلهوسی
ای پسر جام می ام ده که به پیری برسی

Che shekar haast dar in shahr ke ghaane shode and
Shaah baazaane tarighat be maghaame magasi

چه شکرهاست درین شهر که قانع شده اند
شاهبازان طریقت به مقام مگسی

Baa dele khoon shode chon naafe khoshash baayad bood
Harke mash hoore jahaan gasht be moshkin nafasi

با دل خون شده چون نافه خوشش باید بود
هر که مش هوره جهان گشت به مشکین نفسی

Baal bogshaayo safir az shajare toobaa zan
Heyf baashad cho to morghi ke asire ghafasi

بال بگشای و صفیر از شجر طوبی زن
حیف باشد چو تو مرغی که اسیر قفسی

Kaarvaan rafto to dar raahe kamin gaah be khaab
Vah ke bas bikhabar az in hame baange jarasi

کاروان رفت و تو در راه کمینگاه به خواب
وه که بس بی خبر از این همه بانگ جرسی

Lamal bargho menat tore va aanasto behi
Fala alli laka aaten beshehaaben ghabasi

لمع البرق من الطور و انست به
فلعلی لک ات بشهاب قبس

Taa cho mejmar nafasi daamane jaanaan girim
Jaan nahaadim bar aatash ze peye khosh nafasi

تا چو مجمر نفسی دامن جانان گیرم
جان نهادیم بر آتش ز پی خوش نفسی

Chand pooyad be havaaye to ze har soo Hafez
Yassarallaho tarighan beka yaa moltamasi

چند پوید به هوای تو ز هر سو حافظ
یسّر الله طریقا بک یا ملتمسی

I wrote the story of my longing and my eye was weeping,
Come, for from sadness my life is ready to be departing.

In longing for you I told my two eyes frequently,
"O resting place for Salma! Salma[1], where is she?"

A rare and rather extraordinary event this must surely be,
I die from love but my murderer complains about me.

Who has the ability to criticise your gown's purity,
For as the dewdrop on the rose petal is your purity.

From the dust under your foot, tulip and rose got their beauty,
When the creative Pen wrote what's watery and what's dusty.

O Saki arise, the dawn breeze is scattering amber scent,
From the sun soaked vine, bring pure juice with that scent.

Eschew lazy heaviness to gain success! For, the saying is,
"In being sharp and swift the entire traveler's capital is".

Without your fine form there is nothing left that is me,
Only because of your face any good in my life do I see.

How can Hafiz say anything about the beauty of you?
Like God's qualities, you are beyond comprehension too.

(W-C 559)
[1] *"...Salma..." See the notes for W-C 534 above. The first verse and several other lines are in Arabic.*

Katabto ghessata shavghi va madmaee baaki

Biyaa ke bi to be jaan aamadam ze ghamnaaki

كتبت قصّه شوقى و مدمعى باكى

بياكه بى تو به جان آمدم ز غمناكى

Basaa ke gofteam az shovgh baa do dideye khish

Ayaa manaazela salmaa fa ayna salmaaki

بساكه گفته ام از شوق با دو ديده خويش

ايا منازلا سلمى فاين سلماك

Ajib vaaghe-eiyo gharib haadese ist

Anastaberto ghatilan va ghaateli shaaki

عجيب واقعه اى و غريب حادثه ايست

انا اصطبرت قتيلا و قاتلى شاكى

Keraa rasad ke konad eybe daamane paakat

Ke hamcho ghatre ke bar barge gol chekad paaki

كرا رسد كه كند عيب دامن پاكت

كه همچو قطره كه بر برگ گل چكد پاكى

Ze khaake paaye to daad aabe rooye laalevo gol

Cho kelke so-n ragham zad bar aabiyo khaki

ز خاك پاى تو داد آب روى لاله و گل

چو كلك صنع رقم زد بر آبى و خاكى

Sabaa abir feshaan gasht saaghiyaa barkhiz

Va haata shamsata karmen motayyaben zaaki

صبا عبيرفشان گشت ساقيا برخيز

و هات شمسه كرم مطيّب زاكى

Daettakaasola tagh nam faghad jaraa masalon

Ke zaade raah rovaan chosti asto chaalaaki

دع التكاسل تغنم فقد جرى مثل

كه زاد راهروان چستى است و چالاكى

Asar namaand ze man bi shamaayelat aari

Araa ma-aasera mahyaaya men mohayyaaki

اثر نماند ز من بى شمايلت آرى

ارى مآثر محياى من محيّاك

Ze vasfe hosne to Hafez chegoone notgh zanad

Ke chon sefaate elaahi varaaye edraaki

ز وصف حسن تو حافظ چگونه نطق زند

كه چون صفات الهى وراى ادراكى

From the beggar that I am, who will take this message to the kings,
'At the dreg-drinker's feast, for one jar they give two thousand kings'.

Even if that wine is immature, and this associate is one who is mature,
A thousand times is the immature better than a thousand of the mature.

O Sheikh, don't divert me from the path by counting beads on the rosary,
For a bird that has become wise won't fall again into such captivity.

I became ruined and have gained notoriety, but this hope I retain,
That by spiritual attention from dear ones a good name I can attain.

Cast a look on the false gold of our heart, you who sell alchemy,
We have tried to bait a snare, but we have no capital at all really.

To whom should I complain? To whom can I tell the story?
That your lip was our life but in it there was no permanency.

I wonder at the infidelity of the beloved, who gave no greeting,
Who sent no message in a letter and no salaam was penning.

I have the desire to serve you; be my purchaser, don't sell me,
For it is rare that a slave like me gains the fortune of slavery.

Loose the arrow of your eyelash; shed the blood of Hafiz,
For such a killer no one who will take any revenge there is.

(W-C 560) (This Ghazal was not found in Avery or Saberi).

Ke barad be nazde shaahaan ze mane gedaa payaami
Ke be bazme dord nooshaan do hezaar jam be jaami

که برد به نزد شاهان ز من گدا پیامی
که به بزم دردنوشان دوهزار جم به جامی

Agar aan sharaab khaam asto gar in harif pokhte
Be hezaar baare behtar ze hezaar pokhte khaami

اگر آن شراب خام است وگراین حریف پخته
به هزار باره بهتر ز هزار پخته خامی

Ze raham mayafkan ey sheikh be daanehaaye tasbih
Ke cho morgh zairak oftad nafetad be hich daami

ز رهم میفکن ای شیخ به دانه های تسبیح
که چو مرغ زیرک افتد نفتد به هیچ دامی

Shodeam kharaabo bad naamo hanooz omid vaaram
Ke be hemmate azizaan berasam be nik naami

شده ام خراب و بدنام و هنوز امیدوارم
که به همّت عزیزان برسم به نیک نامی

To ke kimiyaa forooshi nazari be ghalbe maa kon
Ke bezaa ati nadaarimo fekande im daami

تو که کیمیا فروشی نظری به قلب ما کن
که بضاعتی نداریم و فکنده ایم دامی

Be kojaa baram shekaayat be ke gooyam in hekaayat
Ke labat hayaate maa boodo nadaashti davaami

به کجا برم شکایت به که گویم این حکایت
که لبت حیات ما بود و نداشتی دوامی

Ajab az vafaaye jaanaan ke tafagh ghodi nafarmood
Na be naamei payaami na be khaamei salaami

عجب از وفای جانان که تفقّدی نفرمود
نه به نامه ای پیامی نه به خامه ای سلامی

Sare khedmate to daaram bekharam be lotfo mafroosh
Ke cho bande kamtar oftad be mobaaraki gholaami

سر خدمت تو دارم بخرم به لطف و مفروش
که چو بنده کمتر افتد به مبارکی غلامی

Begoshaay tire mojgaano beriz khoone Hafez
Ke chonin koshande ee raa nakonad kas enteghaami

بگشای تیر مژگان و بریز خون حافظ
که چنین کشنده ای را نکند کس انتقامی

The people spoke and said that a second Joseph[1] you are,
When I looked carefully I found that better you are.

When you smile you are so sweet it's not enough to say that you are,
The Khusro of beauties; or that the sweet Shirin[2] of this time you are.

One cannot say your mouth is like a rosebud that's not yet open,
For such a delicate mouth as yours the rosebud was never given.

A hundred times your mouth spoke and said you would satisfy me,
Why is it like the free-born lily with your tongue you talk so glibly?

You said you would fulfill my desire, but would also take my life,
I fear you won't give what I want, but you will surely take my life.

Through my life's shield your sultry eye sent an arrow,
Whoever has seen in a languid eye such a mighty bow?

As with a teardrop, you wipe from the sight of everybody,
Anyone that you do not see, even if it's just momentarily.

In the Way, as Hafiz made a foot from his head, like the pen,
Why do you not, from kindness, read him like a letter then?

(W-C 561)
[1] *"..a second Joseph..." A reference to Prophet Joseph (Yusuf) who was renowned, amongst other things, for his physical beauty*
[2] *"...Shirin..." In literature the famously beautiful wife, eventually, of a famous ruler, Khusro. Part of a complex love triangle involving Farhad. Here used as a symbol for female beauty.*

Goftand khalaayegh ke toee yoosofe saani

Chon nik bedidm be haghighat beh az aani

گفتند خلایق که توئی یوسف ثانی

چون نیک بدیدم به حقیقت به از آنی

Shirin taraz aani be shekar khande ke gooyam

Ey khosrove khoobaan ke to shirine zamaani

شیرین تر از آنی به شکر خنده که گویم

ای خسرو خوبان که تو شیرین زمانی

Tashbihe dahaanat natavaan kard be ghonche

Hargez nabovad ghonche bedin tang dahaani

تشبیه دهانت نتوان کرد به غنچه

هرگز نبود غنچه بدین تنگ دهانی

Sad baar begofti ke daham zaan dahanat kaam

Cho soosane aazaade cheraa jomle zabaani

صد بار بگفتی که دهم زان دهنت کام

چون سوسن آزاده چرا جمله زبانی

Gooee bedaham kaamato jaanat besetaanam

Tarsam nadahi kaamamo jaanam besetaani

گویی بدهم کامت و جانت بستانم

ترسم ندهی کامم و جانم بستانی

Chashme to khadang az separe jaan gozaraanad

Bimaar ke didast bedin sakht kamaani

چشم تو خدنگ از سپر جان گذراند

بیمار که دیده ست بدین سخت کمانی

Chon ashk biyan daaziyash az dideye mardom

Aan raa ke dami az nazare khish beraani

چون اشک بیندازی اش از دیده مردم

آنرا که دمی از نظر خویش برانی

Dar raahe to Hafez cho ghalam kard ze sar pay

Chon naame cheraa yek damash az lotf nakhaani

در راه تو حافظ چو قلم کرد ز سر پای

چون نامه چرا یکدمش از لطف نخوانی

Your lip I am kissing: its wine I am drinking,
To the water of life I find that I am reaching.

Your secret mystery I cannot tell to any other,
Nor can I bear that with you there is another.

The cup keeps kissing your lip and blood it is drinking,
The rose keeps seeing your face and profusely sweating.

Bring the wine cup and to Jamshid no attentions pay,
Who knows when Jamshid was; or when was Kay[1]?

O moon maestro, to play on this harp reach out,
Touch the veins so that with them, I may sing out.

Hafiz, for a while, still, tell your tongue to stay,
Hear from the Ney what the tongue-less have to say.

(W-C 562)
[1] *"...Jamshid....Kay..." For Jamshid see the glossary in volume one. Kay – probably referring to a legendary monarch.*

Labash miboosamo dar mikesham mey
Be aabe zendegaani bordeam pey

لبش می بوسم و در می کشم می
به آب زندگانی برده ام پی

Na raazash mitavaanam goft baa kas
Na kas raa mitavaanam did baa vey

نه رازش می توانم گفت با کس
نه کس را می توانم دید با وی

Labash miboosado khoon mikhorad jaam
Rokhash mibinado gol mekonad khey

لبش می بوسد و خون می خورد جام
رخش می بیند و گل می کند خوی

Bede jaame meyo az jam makon yaad
Ke midaanad ke jam key boodo key key

بده جام می و از جم مکن یاد
که می داند که جم کی بود و کی کی

Bezan dar parde chang ey maahe motreb
Ragash bekhraash taa bekhroosham az vey

بزن در پرده چنگ ای ماه مطرب
رگش بخراش تا بخروشم از وی

Zabaanat dar kash ey Hafez zamaani
Hadise bi zabaanaan beshno az ney

زبانت درکش ای حافظ زمانی
حدیث بی زبانان بشنو از نی

I am hung over from wine! O Saki bring more wine,
Fill the cup. Without wine the gathering does not shine.

In the veil, love for that moon-like face cannot be told fully,
Maestro strike up another tune and bring us more wine Saki.

I have taken the form of the door-knocking ring, so that now,
The guard won't drive us from this door to another anyhow.

In wanting to see your face one day, I and hope are uniting.
The hope of union with you fills me with vain dreaming.

I am hung over from those two eyes, is there a cup to be found?
I am sick for those two rubies, is there not an answer to be found?

Hafiz, why give your heart to those images of beauty,
Since when does a mirage satisfy one who is thirsty?

*(W-C 563) The radif here translates into different terms such as "A little wine,"; "A little lustre";
"Another door" & etc.*

Makhmoore jaame eshgham saaghi bede sharaabi

مخمور جام عشقم ساقی بده شرابی

Por kon ghadah ke bi mey majlis nadaarad aabi

پر کن قدح که بی می مجلس ندارد آبی

Vasfe rokhe cho maahash dar parde raast naayad

وصف رخ چو ماهش در پرده راست ناید

Motreb bezan navaaee saaghi bede sharaabi

مطرب بزن نوائی ساقی بده شرابی

Shod halghe ghaamate man taa ba-dazin raghibat

شد حلقه قامت من تا بعد از این رقیبت

Zin dar degar naraanad maa raa be hich baabi

زین در دگر نراند ما را به هیچ بابی

Dar entezaare rooyat mavo omide roozi

در انتظار رویت ما و امید روزی

Dar eshveye vesaalat maavo khiyaale khaabi

در عشوه وصالت ما و خیال خوابی

Makhmoore aan do chashmam ayaa kojaast jaami

مخمور آن دو چشمم آیا کجاست جامی

Bimaare aan do la-lam akher kam az javaabi

بیمار آن دو لعلم آخر کم از جوابی

Hafez che minahi del to dar khiyaale khoobaan

حافظ چه می نهی دل تو در خیال خوبان

Key teshne sir gardad az lameye saraabi

کی تشنه سیر گردد از لمعه سرابی

"Ask for wine and scatter the rose. From time what is your expectation?"
At dawn the rose said to the bulbul, "What do you say about this notion?"

Take the divan cushion to the garden, so of the beloved and Saki as well,
You may taste the lip, kiss the cheek, drink the wine, and the rose smell.

Walk tall as a box tree and straight into the garden be striding,
So the cypress, on seeing your stature, may learn heart-catching.

The smile of your rosebud brings fortune; let's see to whom.
O branch of the beautiful rosebush you grow for whom.

In the path of the wind stands the candle of beauty,
Try to profit from the capital of a face full of beauty.

Today when the bazaar is busy with the bustle of noisy buying,
Find and store up from the stock of virtue what's worth having.

A hundred musk pods of China are in every ringlet of that hair,
It would have been good if the perfume of kindness was there.

In the king's garden, with a song, is every bird that enters there,
The bulbul with a fine melody, and Hafiz chanting a prayer.

(W-C 564) See the various symbols of the garden in the appendix of book one.

Mey khaaho gol afshaan kon az dahr che mijooee
In goft sahar gah gol bolbol to che migooee

می خواه و گل افشان کن از دهر چه می جوی
این گفت سحرگه گل بلبل تو چه می گوی

Masnad be golestaan bar taa shaahedo saaghi raa
Lab giriyo rokh boosi mey nooshiyo gol booee

مسند به گلستان بر تا شاهد و ساقی را
لب گیری و رخ بوسی می نوشی و گل بوی

Shemshaad kharaamaan kon vaahange golestaan kon
Taa sarv biyaamoozad az ghadde to del jooee

شمشاد خرامان کن واهنگ گلستان کن
تا سرو بیاموزد از قدّ تو دلجوی

Taa ghoncheye khandaanat dovlat be ke khaahad daad
Ey shaakhe gole ranaa az bahre ke mirooee

تا غنچه خندانت دولت به که خواهد داد
ای شاخ گل رعنا از بهر که می روی

Chon sha-m nekoo rooee dar rahgozare baad ast
Tarfe honari bar band az sham e nekoo rooee

چون شمع نکورویی برهگذر باد است
طرف هنری بربند از شمع نکورویی

Emrooz ke baazaarat por jooshe kharidaar ast
Daryaabo beneh ganji az maayeye nikooee

امروز که بازارت پر جوش خریدار است
دریاب و بنه گنجی از مایه نیکویی

Aan torre ke har ja-dash sad naafeye chin daarad
Khosh boodi agar boodi booeesh ze khosh khooee

آن طرّه که هر جعدش صد نافه چین دارد
خوش بودی اگر بودی بویش ز خوشخویی

Har morgh be dastaani dar golshane shaah aayad
Bolbol be navaasaazi Hafez be doaa gooee

هر مرغ به دستانی در گلشن شاه آید
بلبل به نواسازی حافظ به دعا گویی

Spring has arrived! Try hard so that full of its joys you may be,
Many roses will bloom again but under the rose bed you may be.

The hidden harp is giving out good advice continually,
But you benefit from it only when you are really ready.

I don't tell you what to drink or with whom to sit,
If you are bright and learned you already know it.

In the book of the meadow every leaf tells of a different state,
It would be very sad if you were to be unaware of every state.

Though the way from us to the friend a fearful one may be,
It's quite easy going if with the stages you have familiarity[1].

The cash of your life, excessive worldly worries steal away,
If in this complex story you are engaged night and day.

O Hafiz, if from your high fortune help there should be,
You will be hunted by the beloved with many a fine quality[2].

(W-C 565)

[1] "...stages..." The Sufi path has both transient 'states' and permanent 'stages'. An example of a stage would be Repentance, Trust, Permanence, Perfection & etc. The states mentioned in the previous verse include such temporary experiences as weeping, turning in ecstasy & etc...

[2] "...many a fine quality..." The Beloved, God, has many beautiful Names or qualities. At a certain level the seeker may become the sought.

Nov bahaar ast dar aan koosh ke khosh del baashi

Ke basi gol bedamad baazo to dar gel baashi

نوبهار است در آن کوش که خوشدل باشی

که بسی گل بدمد باز و تو در گل باشی

Change dar parde hamin midahadat pand vali

Vazat aangaah konad sood ke ghaabel baashi

چنگ در پرده همین می دهدت پند ولی

وعظت آنگاه کند سود که قابل باشی

Man nagooyam ke konoon baa ke neshino che benoosh

Ke to khod daani agar zirako aaghel baashi

من نگویم که کنون با که نشین و چه بنوش

که تو خود دانی اگر زیرک و عاقل باشی

Dar chaman har varaghi daftare haali degar ast

Heyf baashad ke ze haale hame ghaafel baashi

در چمن هر ورقی دفتر حالی دگر است

حیف باشد که ز حال همه غافل باشی

Garche raahist por az bim ze maa taa bare doost

Raftan aasaan bovad ar vaaghefe manzel baashi

گرچه راهیست پر از بیم ز ما تا بر دوست

رفتن آسان بود ار واقف منزل باشی

Naghde omrat bebarad ghosseye donyaa be gazaaf

Gar shabo rooz darin ghesseye moshkel baashi

نقد عمرت ببرد غصّه دنیا به گزاف

گر شب و روز درین قصّه مشکل باشی

Hafezaa gar madad az bakhte bolandat baashad

Seyde aan shaahede matboo shamaayel baashi

حافظا گر مدد از بخت بلندت باشد

صید آن شاهد مطبوع شمایل باشی

O breeze of a happy dawn for the sign that well you know,
Go to the street of that one at the time that well you know.

You carry news of seclusion's secret; the eye is looking for you,
Not by command but with insight into man, go in the way you know.

Say that my feeble life is not under my control; for the sake of God,
Give from that soul-refreshing ruby lip that which well you know.

These two words I wrote so that a stranger could not understand them,
You too be so kind as to read them in the way that you know.

With us the image of your sword is of one thirsting for water,
You have got your captive, kill in the way that only you know.

How should I not fasten my hope to your gold woven cummerbund,
Oh you beauty! In that waist there is a precise point that well you know.

Hafiz, in this business Turkish and Arabic are as one,
Tell the story of love in the language which well you know.

(W-C 566) The radif here is "That you know". We have used "You know"

Nasime sobhe sa-aadat bedaan neshaan ke to daani
Gozar be kooye folaan kon dar aan zamaan ke to daani

نسیم صبح سعادت بدان نشان که تو دانی
گذر به کوی فلان کن در آن زمان که تو دانی

To peyke khalvate raaziyyo dide bar sare raahat
Be mardomi na be farmaan chonaan beraan ke to daani

تو پیک خلوت رازیّ و دیده بر سر راهت
به مردمی نه به فرمان چنان بران که تو دانی

Begoo ke jaane zaeefam ze dast raft khodaa raa
Ze la-le rooh fazaayash bebakhsh azaan ke to daani

بگو که جان ضعیفم ز دست رفت خدارا
ز لعل روح فزایش ببخش از آن که تو دانی

Man in do harf nebeshtam chonaan ke gheir nadaanest
To ham ze rooye keraamat chonaan bekhaan ke to daani

من این دو حرف نبشتم چنانکه غیر ندانست
تو هم ز روی کرامت چنان بخوان که تو دانی

Khiyaale tighe to baa maa hadise teshnevo aabast
Asire khish gerefti bekosh chonaan ke to daani

خیال تیغ تو با ما حدیث تشنه و آب است
اسیر خویش گرفتی بکش چنانکه تو دانی

Omid dar kamare zar kashat chegoone nabandam
Daghigheist negaaraa dar aan miyaan ke to daani

امید در کمر زرکشت چگونه نبندم
دقیقه ایست نگارا در آن میان که تو دانی

Yekist torkiyo taazi dar in moaamele Hafez
Hadise eshgh bayaan kon bedaan zabaan ke to daani

یکیست ترکی و تازی درین معامله حافظ
حدیث عشق بیان کن بدان زبان که تو دانی

Take wine and from a great big cup drink it,
So that you can uproot the heart's grief with it.

Like a great dish of wine keep the heart wide open,
How long, in a jug will you keep it corked up then?

When of selflessness, deep and long you are drinking,
Of your own self much less will you feel like boasting.

Be like the stone at your foot, not like vapour in the sky,
Your robe is a mixture[1] of the colours of corruption's dye.

Bind your heart to wine, and like a true man be[2],
One who breaks the neck of piety and hypocrisy.

Get up and make an effort like Hafiz, so that maybe,
One throwing their self at the beloved's feet you'll be.

(W-C 567)

[1] "..Your robe is a mixture..." Man for the most part consists of a mixture of good and bad,

[2] "...like a true man be..." The holy Qur'an has a verse that declares that man was made in the best of moulds but has become the lowest of the low. Sura 95; 4 & 5.

Noosh kon jaame sharaabe yek mani

Taa bedaan bikhe gham az del bar kani

نوش کن جام شراب یک منی

تا بدان بیخ غم از دل برکنی

Del goshaade daar chon jaame sharaab

Sar gerefte chand chon khomme dani

دل گشاده دار چون جام شراب

سرگرفته چند چون خمّ دنی

Chon ze jaame bikhodi ratli kashi

Kam zani az khishtan laafe mani

چون ز جام بیخودی رطلی کشی

کم زنی از خویشتن لاف منی

Sangsaan sho dar ghadam ni hamcho abr

Jomle rangaamiziyo tar daamani

سنگ سان شو در قدم نی همچو ابر

جمله رنگ آمیزی و تر دامنی

Del be mey dar band taa mardaane vaar

Gardane saalooso taghvaa beshkani

دل به می در بند تا مردانه وار

گردن سالوس و تقوی بشکنی

Khizo jahdi kon cho Hafez taa magar

Khishtan dar paaye mashoogh afkani

خیز و جهدی کن چو حافظ تا مگر

خویشتن در پای معشوق افکنی

As far as you can, get from time whatever in it there is,
O my very life cherish this moment, the fruit of life it is.

For granting desires, the turning sphere holds life in pledge to be,
Strive to get the most you can of joyful ease from destiny.

Hear the advice of lovers and make joy the door you pass through,
For of no value is the business that in the transitory world you do.

To one of puritan disposition, don't speak of the way of the Rend,
For the doctor who's not a confidant, hidden pain can't apprehend.

When I pass on from here, gardener, may the law say forbidden it is,
That in my plot of earth you plant any cypress that not the friend is.

O sweet-mouthed one, night-riser's supplications do not try fighting,
For the seal ring of Solomon the one great Name[1] is protecting.

My beloved Joseph has gone! O brothers have some pity,
The wondrous state of the elder of Canaan, grief has shown me[2].

The barrel busting guardian does not know, for the Sufi,
A homemade thing is like a pomegranate red ruby.

You go, and the blood of the people your eyelashes have shed,
Beloved so fast and furiously you go, you might be left stranded.

Though from the arrow of your eye my heart I guarded,
Your eyebrow's bow still steals it from the forehead.

With a little kindness concentrate the fragmented heart[3] of Hafiz,
You whose hair curl the gathering point for the dispersed one is.

A desire for wine will put an end to the remorseful puritan,
Do nothing that will bring you remorse then, O wise man.

O stony-hearted beauty, if for us you have no consideration,
Then to the second Asaf[4] I will go and explain my situation.

(W-C 568)

[1] "...Solomon the one great Name..." A reference to the 'Isme Azam', the great and unknown Name of Allah, with which Prophet Solomon was able to control all kinds of good or bad spirits.
[2] This verse refers to the story of Prophet Joseph, Yusuf, whose brothers threw him into a well, and whose father Prophet Jacob (Yaqub) grieved so strongly for that he lost his sight.
[3] "...concentrate the fragmented heart..." The gathering of the heart is meditation used by Sufis. The next line suggests the gathering point is the curl of the beloved's hair.
[4] "...Asaf..." See glossary in volume one.

Vaght raa ghanimat daan aan ghadar ke betvaani
Haasel az hayaat ey jaan in dam ast taa daani

وقت را غنیمت دان آنقدر که بتوانی
حاصل از حیات ای جان این دم است تا دانی

Kaam bakhshiye gardoon omr dar avaz daarad
Jahd kon ke az dovlat daade eysh bestaani

کام بخشی گردون عمر در عوض دارد
جهد کن که از دولت داد عیش بستانی

Pande aasheghaan beshno vaz dare tarab baaz aay
Kin hame nemiarzad shoghle aalame faani

پند عاشقان بشنو وز در طرب باز آی
کاین همه نمی ارزد شغل عالم فانی

Pishe zaahed az rendi dam mazan ke natvaan goft
Baa tabibe naa mahram haale darde penhaani

پیش زاهد از رندی دم مزن که نتوان گفت
با طبیب نامحرم حال درد پنهانی

Baaghbaan cho man zinjaa bogzaram haraamat baad
Gar be jaaye man sarvi gheyre doost benshaani

باغبان چو من زینجا بگذرم حرامت باد
گر به جای من سروی غیر دوست بنشانی

Baa doaaye shab khizaan ey shekar dahaan mastiz
Dar panaahe yek esmast khaatame soleymaani

با دعای شب خیزان ای شکر دهان مستیز
در پناه یک اسم است خاتم سلیمانی

Yoosofe azizam raft ey baraadarran rahmi
Kaz ghamash ajab didam haale pire kan aani

یوسف عزیزم رفت ای برادران رحمی
کز غمش عجب دیدم حال پیر کنعانی

Khom shekan nemidaanad in ghadar ke soofi raa
Jense khaanegi baashad hamcho la-le rommaani

خم شکن نمی داند این قدر که صوفی را
جنس خانگی باشد همچو لعل رمّانی

Miraviyyo mojgaanat khoone khalgh mirizad
Tiz miravi jaanaa tarsamat foroo maani

می رویّ و مژگانت خون خلق می ریزد
تیز می روی جانا ترسمت فرو مانی

Del ze naavake chashmat goosh daashtam likan
Abrooye kamaan daarat mibarad be pishaani

دل ز ناوک چشمت گوش داشتم لیکن
ابروی کماندارت می برد به پیشانی

Jam kon be ehsaani Hafeze parishaan raa
Ey shekanje gisooyat majmae parishaani

جمع کن به احسانی حافظ پریشان را
ای شکنج گیسویت مجمع پریشانی

Zaahede pashimaan raa zovghe baade khaahad kosht
Aaghelaa makon kaari kaavarad pashimaani

زاهد پشیمان را ذوق باده خواهد کشت
عاقلا مکن کاری کاورد پشیمانی

Gar to faareghi az maa ey negaare sangin del
Haale khod bekhaaham goft pishe aasafe saani

گر تو فارغی از ما ای نگار سنگین دل
حال خود بخواهم گفت پیش آصف ثانی

Love of my life, I am an admirer; I know you know this,
For you see what is unseen and read what not written is.

Of lover and beloved the blame-giver knows what exactly?
The blind eye sees not, and of these hidden mysteries, especially.

Toss your hair with abandon so that the Sufi dances and jumps about,
And from each of the patches on his robe a thousand idols will fall out.

The solution to the affairs of the desiring is in that heart-holding eyebrow,
Sit awhile with us for God's sake and undo the knot of your own brow[1].

Angels prostrating to Adam[2] resolved to kiss the ground under you,
For they found more than the quality of man in the beauty of you.

From the hair of beauties comes breeze that our eye's lamp is lighting,
O Lord, may the dispersing wind never bring sorrow to this gathering.

So sad, that the joy of sitting up all night, with dawn breeze, dozed!
O heart, you only appreciate the time of union when it has passed.

To be annoyed with travelling companions is not for a real traveler,
Endure hardships of this stage by recalling when things were easier.

Hafiz, you're entranced, imagining that in that one's hair a ring you see,
Make sure you're not the ring-knocker on the door of impossible felicity.

(W-C 569) The radif here translates into different terms such as "You know"; "You read"; "Human" & etc.

[1] *"...undo the knot..." Whilst the spiritual heart is traditionally identified with the location of the physical heart in the chest, for many Sufis it is identified with the brow.*

[2] *"...Angels prostrating to Adam..." The holy Qur'an tells the story of the angels who were told to prostrate to the first man, Adam. They all did so with the exception of Satan (Shaitan).*

Havaa khaahe toam jaanaavo midaanam ke midaani
Ke ham naadide mibiniyyo ham nanveshte mikhaani

هواخواه توأم جانا و می دانم که می دانی
که هم نادیده می بینیّ و هم ننوشته می خوانی

Malaamat goo che dar yaabad miyaane aashegho mashoogh
Nabinad chashme naa binaa khosoos asraare penhaani

ملامت گو چه در یابد میان عاشق و معشوق
نبیند چشم نابینا خصوص اسرار پنهانی

Biyafshaan zolfo soofi raa be paa baaziyyo raghs aavar
Kea z har rogh e ye dalghash hezaaraan bot biyaf shaani

بیفشان زلف و صوفی را پابازیّ و رقص آور
که از هر رقعه دلقش هزاران بت بیفشانی

Goshaade kaare mosh taaghaan dar aan abrooye del bandast
Khodaa raa yek nafas benshin gereh bog shaa ze pishaani

گشاد کار مشتاقان در آن ابروی دلبند است
خدا را یک نفس بنشین گره بگشا ز پیشانی

Malak dar sajdeye aadam zamin boose to niyyat kard
Ke dar hosne to chizi yaaft bish az tovre ensaani

ملک در سجده آدم زمین بوس تو نیّت کرد
که در حسن تو چیزی یافت بیش از طور انسانی

Cheraagh afrooze chashme maa nasime zolfe khoobaan ast
Mabaad in ja-m raa yaa rab gham az baade parishaani

چراغ افروز چشم ما نسیم زلف خوبان است
مباد این جمع را یارب غم از باد پریشانی

Darighaa eyshe shab giri ke dar khaabe sahar bogzasht
Nadaani ghadre vaght ey del magar vaghti ke dar maani

دریغا عیش شبگیری که در خواب سحر بگذشت
ندانی قدر وقت ای دل مگر وقتی که درمانی

Malool az hamrahaan boodan tarighe kaaravaani nist
Bekash dosh vaariye manzel be yaade ahde aasaani

ملول از همرهان بودن طریق کاروانی نیست
بکش دشواری منزل به یاد عهد آسانی

Khiyaale chambare zolfash faribat midahad Hafez
Negar taa halgheye eghbaale naa momken najom baani

خیال چنبر زلفش فریبت می دهد حافظ
نگر تا حلقه اقبال ناممکن نجنبانی

A thousand efforts I made so that my beloved you would be,
So that one who grants my excited heart's desire you would be.

As the lamp that keeps my eye watchful at night, be,
So the comforter of my hopeful heart you would be.

When kings of beautiful mien treat slaves kindly,
Amongst them my lord and master you would be.

By that cornelian[1] mouth that makes my heart so bloody,
If I make complaint the keeper of this secret you will be.

In the meadow idols hand in hand with lovers see,
If this were possible for you, my idol you would be.

For me the rays of the sun would be a meager quarry,
If for one moment a deer such as you my prey would be.

Three kisses from your two lips you have promised me,
If these are not forthcoming in my debt you will be.

The desire I have is that one midnight it may come to be,
Instead of having tears in my lap, in your embrace I will be.

Though the Hafiz[2] of the city, I am not worth a grain of barley,
Unless from your beneficence my beloved you would be.

(W-C 570) The radif here is mostly "You shall be" or "You should be". We have used "Would be".
[1] "...cornelian..." This is a red stone. It is its redness that is referred to here.
[2] "...the hafiz..." This means guardian, either in the more general sense or in the sense of being one who preserves the holy Qur'an by being able to recite it by heart – which was the case with Hafiz.

Hezaar jahd bekardam ke yaare man baashi

Moraad bakh she dele bi gharaare man baashi

هزار جهد بکردم که یار من باشی

مرادبخش دل بیقرار من باشی

Cheraaghe dideye shab zende daare man gardi

Anise khaatere ammid vaare man baashi

چراغ دیده شب زنده دار من گردی

انیس خاطر امیدوار من باشی

Cho khosrovaane malaahat be bandegaan naazand

To dar miyaane khodaa vandegaare man baashi

چو خسروان ملاحت به بندگان نازند

تو در میانه خداوندگار من باشی

Az aan aghigh ke khoonin delam ze eshveye ou

Agar konam gelei raaz daare man baashi

از آن عقیق که خونین دلم ز عشوه او

اگر کنم گله ای رازدار من باشی

Dar aan chaman ke botaan daste aasheghaan girand

Garat ze dast bar aayad negaare man baashi

در آن چمن که بتان دست دلبران گیرند

گرت ز دست برآید نگار من باشی

Shavad ghazaaleye khorshid seyde laaghare man

Gar aahooee cho to yek dam shekaare man baashi

شود غزاله خورشید صید لاغر من

گر آهوئی چو تو یکدم شکار من باشی

Se boose kaz do labat kardei vazifeye man

Agar adaa nakoni gharz dare man baashi

سه بوسه کز دو لبت کرده ای وظیفه من

اگر ادا نکنی قرض دار من باشی

Man in moraad bebinam be khod ke nim shabi

Be jaaye ashke ravaan dar kenaare man baashi

من این مراد ببینم به خود که نیم شبی

به جای اشک روان در کنار من باشی

Man arche Hafeze shahram jovi nemi arzam

Magar to az karame khish yaare man baashi

من ارچه حافظ شهرم جوی نمی ارزم

مگر تو از کرم خویش یار من باشی

O mouth! A treasure chest of pearls you appear to be,
O Lord! So fitting the crescent line around it seems to be.

Now the idea of union seems but a pleasant deception,
Let us see what imagery is displayed by the imagination.

Heart departed; eye bloody; broken body; life gone;
In such close succession love's wonders follow on.

Wine! Though a black slate for the world's sins I may be,
Yet how should one not have hope of the eternal Mercy.

Saki bring a cup, and from seclusion's hideaway withdraw me,
So I may go to many a tavern door and a carefree wine drinker be.

Don't let go of these four things if you are wise and learned,
Safety, pure wine, the beloved, and a place that's deserted.

Since the turning of times wheel is never ceasing,
Hafiz, no complaints! Let us get on with wine drinking.

In the time of the Asaf[1] of this age the heart's cup has purity,
Arise then and wine purer than the clearest water give to me.

Due to his efforts and good fortune the country is rejoicing,
O Lord, forever may this honour and splendour be lasting.

The throne of splendour and honour, the mine of power and authority,
The evidence of the religion and the country – Abu Nasr Abu'l-Mali[2].

(W-C 571) There are six additional verses from W-C in the appendix.
  [1] *"...Asaf..." See glossary in volume one.*
  [2] *"...Abu Nasr Abu'l-Mali..."A famed poet (W-C pp 928) or a ruler according to Avery pp546.*

Yaa mab saman yohaaki dorjan menal leaali

يا مبسما يحاكى درجا من اللالى

Yaa rab che dar khor aamad gerdash khate helaali

يا رب چه در خور آمد گردش خط هلالى

Haali khiyaale vaslat khosh midahad faribam

حالى خيال وصلت خوش مى دهد فريبم

Taa khod che naghsh baazad in soorate khiyaali

تا خود چه نقش بازد اين صورت خيالى

Del rafto dide khoon shod tan khasto jaan boroon shod

دل رفت و ديده خون شد تن خست و جان برون شد

Fel eshgh mo-jebaaton ya-tina bet tavaali

فى العشق معجبات ياتين بالتوالى

Mey deh ke garche gashtam naame siyaahe aalam

مى ده که گرچه گشتم نامه سياه عالم

Nomid key tavaan bood az lotfe laa yazaali

نوميد کى توان بود از لطف لايزالى

Saaghi biyaar jaami vaz khalvatam boroon kash

ساقى بيار جامى وز خلوتم برون کش

Taa dar be dar begardam ghallaasho laa obaali

تا دربدر بگردم قلّاش و لا ابالى

Az chaar chiz magzar gar aagheliyyo zirak

از چار چيز مگذر گر عاقلى و زيرک

Amno sharaabe bi ghash mashoogho jaaye khaali

امن و شراب بى غش معشوق و جاى خالى

Chon nist naghshe dovraan dar hich haal saabet

چون نيست نقش دوران در هيچ حال ثابت

Hafez makon shekaayat taa mey khorim haali

حافظ مکن شکايت تا مى خوريم حالى

Saafist jaame khaater dar dovre aasafe ahd

صافيست جام خاطر در دور آصف عهد

Ghom fasgheni rahighan asfaa menaz zolali

قم فاسقنى رحيقا اصفى من الزلال

Al molko ghad tabaahaa men jaddehi va jedda

الملک قد تباهى من جدّه و جدّه

Yaa rab ke jaavdaan baad in ghadro in ma-aali

يا رب که جاودان باد اين قدر و اين معالى

Masnad forooze dovlat kaane shokooho shovkat

مسند فروز دولت کان شکوه و شوکت

Borhaane molko mellat boo nasre bol ma aali

برهان ملک و ملّت بونصر بوالمعالى

With two locks of hair Salma[1] holds my heart in captivity,
Each and every day my soul is crying out to me.

To a heart-lost one like me, for God's sake show mercy,
And in spite of enemies united with my beloved let me be.

Cynical about my love for Salma you may be,
But first her face you should have seen clearly.

Totally surrender your heart to the beloved so that like me,
You are drowned in love and in the ocean of loving will be.

There is no other way, this heart's grief you must experience,
Otherwise from what you see no joy will you experience.

O beloved, midst the grief of love for you,
In the Lord of the devotees trust we do.

If in us you have observed the least fault or discourtesy,
Penitence at your feet we endure so that pardon there will be.

To the curl of your hair Hafiz's heart went,
In the darkness of night guidance Allah sent.

(W-C 572)
  [1] "...Salma..." A famed Arabian beauty, used here to imply the Beloved.

Sabat salmaa be sod ghihaa fo aadi
Va roohi kolla yav men li yo naadi

سبت سلمی بصدغیها فوأدی
و روحی کل یوم لی ینادی

Khodaa raa bar mane bidel bebakh shay
Va vaaselni alaa ragh mel a aadi

خدا را بر من بیدل ببخشای
و واصلنی علی رغم الاعادی

Aman ankar tani an eshghe salmaa
Taz avval aan rooye neh koo be vaadi

امن انکرتنی عن عشق سلمی
تز اوّل آن روی نهکو بوادی

Ke hamchon mot be boo tan del va ee rah
Gharighol eshghe fi bahrel vedaadi

که همچون مت ببو تن دل وای ره
غریق العشق فی بحر الوداد

Ghame in del bevaatet khord naa chaar
Va ghar na ou beni aan chet na shaadi

غم این دل بواتت خورد ناچار
و غرنه او بنی آنچت نشادی

Negaaraa dar ghame sovdaay eshghat
Tavakkalnaa alaa rabel ebaadi

نگارا در غم سودای عشقت
توکلنا علی ربّ العباد

Be pey maachaan gharaamat bes pori man
Gharat yek vey raveshti az emaadi

بپی ماچان غرامت بسپرمن
غرت یک وی روشتی از امادی

Dele Hafez shod andar chine zolfat
Be laylen mozlemen vallaaho haadi

دل حافظ شد اندر چین زلفت
بلیل مظلم والله هادی

Glossary 1 Some Symbols

Garden

The cypress tree – slender, upright, elegant, singular and like the letter Alif (a single vertical line in Farsi). It represents the rectitude of the Sheykh not merely in the moral sense, but in the inner and outer posture. To sit in meditation upright, from within, reflecting perhaps the idea of the Qutub – the spiritual pole or axis around which the universe revolves.

The rosebud – the, as yet, not fully realised spiritual potential of the seeker on the way.

The rose – the centripetal manifesting power of God, the Beloved, or the human heart. Its scent is spirit; its centre the essence; its petals the manifesting of God or the opening of the human heart. It is an object for practising concentration by the Sufis.

The bulbul (nightingale) – the lover of the rose and in some respects the voice of the rose. The rose is silent, appearing aloof, whilst the lover is full of extravagant expressions. It is the manifestation of The Word in words. Inwardly, in meditation, it refers to ideas or thoughts arising in the conscious mind from deep inside.

The breeze – consists of intimations or voices from the unseen dimension; or the flow of spiritual energy that inspires the dance in the Sufis. It also carries the connotation of the Nafas ar-Rehman (the breath of the merciful) which is referred to in Hadiths.

The fountain – the source of purification through tears. Weeping is a recognised state amongst Sufis arising from being in touch with the essence of deep seated emotions such as sorrow. It also indicates the generosity and abundance of Allah.

The Body

Head – in man his highest selfhood which must be abased before the Divinity (submission).

Hair - is manifestation of unity into diversity. The curls may refer to the spiralling patterns of the Spirit's energy whose compelling movements the mystic becomes caught up in when 'dancing'..

Face - 'Everything vanishes but His Face'(Qur'an); therefore it refers to the Eternal Divinity. The field of Absolute Existence in the most comprehensive sense; on which various features are identified. It could be described as the substance of the spiritual Essence.

Mole - Mystically it is the single point of unity encompassing all creation.

Eye – if used in the singular we take it to mean perception. Sometimes called the window to the soul. The pupil is said to stand in the same relation to the eye as the perfect man does to God (see Avery pp 109).

Eyelash – beauty that wounds the heart.

Lip – essence of Divinity. Ecstacy.

Waist - the bridge between the higher nature and the lower nature of man.

Hand - control. God says in the Qur'an *'I become My servant's hand and foot'* meaning God controls him.

Feet – As above, but also the lowest part, therefore to point one's feet towards something sacred is a sign of disrespect. To kiss someone's foot a sign of veneration for that person.

Glossary 2

Alphabetic reference to terms found in the text of the ghazals.
gh = ghazal number in this edition

Ad (and Samud); tribes spoken of in the holy Qur'an who were punished for disbelief and persecution of their Prophets.

Adab; good manners – this has a subtle implication indicating that behaviour to others should be refined and spiritually punctilious and pure. For example it would be bad manners to remind someone of a favour given or to sit with one's feet pointing towards Kaaba or the shrine of a saint or to give a thing with ostentation. The demonstration of good manners is considered to reflect the inner state of the person. It can be far more subtle than this – for example the bad thought that a murid might get about the sheikh is poor manners. Extreme refinement of subtle Adab is a preoccupation amongst Sufis. It is also the greeting used to non Muslims rather than asalaam aleikum, which is used between Muslims.

Allah; the Arabic word for God. Sometimes this is translated as the Essence or as The (only) God. Allah and God and the Divinity are used as interchangeable words in this volume.

Allahu Akbar; gh35: 'Greatness belongs to God': the first words (repeated four times) of the call to prayer in Islam.

Alast; many ghazals: A 'day' described as being outside of phenomenal time and space, in which Allah asks the first-created pure un-embodied souls created from the Nur–i-Muhammed' (Logos) –"Am I not your Lord?" To which the souls reply, 'YES'. It is the distant 'remembrance' of this day by the embodied souls that has been said to be the cause of the ecstasy in Sama (music concert) of the Sufis. (See Quran 7:172).

Aloes wood; gh93: incense obtained from wood resin, thought to have medicinal properties and widely used in religious ceremonies.

Anka/Anqa; many ghazals: King of birds – used to symbolise the Beloved or God. Located, according to Fariduddin Attar, on the mysterious Mount Kaf

Ambergris; gh 22: a grey sweet smelling substance used for fixing perfumes.

Arch; 'The heart of those following the *haqiqa*t, when it is tuned and turned towards the real purpose it is called an arch by the enlightened ones' - Khwaja

Muinuddin Hasan Chishti, in *'Meditations of Khwaja Muinuddin Hasan Chishti.; Sharib Press 1992.*

Arghavan; gh16: A purple-pink/reddish flower, also known as 'redbud' (*Cercis Siliquastrum*) or the Judas tree.

Asaf; gh 20, 36: advisor (vizier) to Prophet (King) Solomon. He was scolded by an ant for not seeking earnestly enough the great seal ring lost for a while to Solomon. Used as the exemplar of the wise advisor.

Ashura; gh 16: tenth night of the Muslim month of Muharrem, and one of particular grieving and melancholy for Muslims marking the martyrdom of the son of Hazrat Ali, Imam Hussein.

Ayaz; gh87: Minister of King Mahmud, the bond of affection between them is famous.

Babylon; gh83: an ancient city associated with magic.

Beloved; many ghazals: God, Allah, or the murshid (spiritual guide), or a human beloved (male or female according to context and also used ambiguously as Hafiz writes on many levels at the same time. It is said the Sufis talk outwardly of God or Allah, but inwardly address the Divinity as the Beloved or Friend. The implication in Hafiz will depend on the context and may vary within one ghazal.

Blue-garmented; gh 139: outwardly pious (but inwardly black-hearted). Hypocrites.

Blood Price; gh 84: Money paid to relatives after a murder of one of the family. This indemnifies those who pay from revenge attacks.

Bokhara (and Samarqand); gh 8: Two prominent Persian cities famed for learning and culture; symbolic here possibly of this world and the next.

Breeze; many ghazals: Usually Saba – the soft dawn breeze; a kind of zephyr; the messenger to and from the Beloved; spiritual intuition.

Bulbul; gh30: The nightingale; a bird carrying news of events to the rose (the beloved). The archetype of the lover.

Chashm; gh 136: Literally 'by (or on) my eye' meaning to agree to do something.

Chaugan: gh2; a mallet (probably with a hollow curve) used to play a game on horseback – the origin of modern polo. To be the ball in the game may be symbolic of accepting the' back and forth' of destiny. Also refers to the arch of the eyebrow metaphorically, and thus to the prayer arch.

Cheek; many ghazals: The divine splendour, beauty or glory. Manifestation of the Divine Essence (Avery).

Civit; gh23: small lithe cat-like animal,

Clay; many ghazals: Basic human (animal) nature consisting of savage instincts such as lust, anger, greed etc.

Corner-sitter; many ghazals: One who sits in the corner of the tavern – a reclusive mystic. A corner can in this context also refer to a place where mystics meet informally as distinct from the formal Sufi hospices. Zawiya.

Croesus; an ancient king fabled for his vast wealth.

Daughter of the vine; many ghazals: Wine.

Day of Awakening; gh3; The Last Judgement.

Day of Alast/Azal; see under Alast

Dervish; many ghazals: generally taken to be synonymous with 'Sufi', but it actually is more properly used to denote a Sufi of high degree and one who has no care for the world whatsoever. Feared and venerated for the power to bless or curse.

Dimple (of the chin): gh2; often seen as a pit or well (connotes also the well of prophet Joseph) into which the lover may fall from desire for the beloved's beauty.

Down (Khatt); many ghazals: the fine face hair. Also the newly sprouted hair on an adolescent boy's face presaging the growth of a beard. In many styles of eastern art female beauty may be depicted with a fine shadow to emphasise the roundness of the face. Mystically this can refer to the integration of the spiritual with the material reality. That absolute clarity of detail that takes one beyond imagining. It has the quality of being a border or frame for beauty of the face. The Farsi word can also mean writing.

Dust on the head of...; many ghazals: making something worthless.

Eid-ul-Fitr; gh113: literally breaking the soil (as when a plant emerges from the ground). The Islamic day of festivity following the fasting month of Ramadan. It commences with the sighting of the new moon of the month of Eid.

Eye (on my eye or by my eye); see under 'Chashm'. 'Narcissus eye' – see under narcissus. See under 'Symbols' page 328.

Farhad; gh 129: The Persian lover whose love for his beloved Shirin inspired many Farsi poets! Given an impossible task to carve stairs out of hard rock on nearly completing it he was falsely informed she had died. (see also Shirin).

Fana; Extinction. The state in which the individuality of the Sufi is merged into a Greater Reality so as to be almost indistinguishable from it. What remains of the individuality forms the basis for another state called Baqa (survival). The classic description of this is of a man attending his own funeral. The corpse is Fana the man attending is Baqa,

Fatiha; gh100: The 'oft- repeated' seven opening verses of the holy Qur'an. It is recited as part of the Muslim ritual prayer. It is recited by pilgrims to sacred tombs and on all other religious occasions.

Faqir; gh 139: Poor – it implies Muslim saints of material poverty and great spiritual wealth; wandering Dervishes who depend on alms for living; associated with complete humility.

Girdle; gh 69: symbol of Christianity – usually a chain worn round the waist. It is treated as a symbol of disbelief in the religion of Islam.

Goglet; gh 93: long necked traditional jug for pouring wine. Symbolically may be the spiritual guide, or the holy Prophet Muhammed.

Halwa; many ghazals: Sweetmeats or a sweet dessert.

Hair (or tress)/Zulf; many ghazals: may be understood in many ways such as symbolising the many and varied strands or modes of life which have a single underlying unity - the multiplicity of Divine manifestation. Its other functions in the poems include: veiling the beloved's face; guarding the beloved's face; as a rope for the aspiring lover; as darkness of disbelief or as darkness of non-existence.

Hoopoe; many ghazals: Lapwing. The small crested bird that carried a message from Solomon to the Queen of Sheba (Bilqis queen of Saba). Sometimes used to symbolise the guide (as in Attar's 'Conference of the Birds'). It is referred to in the holy Qur'an.

Harut; gh83: one of two fallen angel associated with magic in Babylon. (the other is Marut).

Hajji Khivam; gh3: can be understood to be obliquely referring to God; The Murshid; or literally to a minister to Abu Ishaq (d 1353). Hajji is one who has performed the Hajj pilgrimage to Mecca.

Hejaz (Hijaz); gh122: That part of Saudi Arabia in which Mecca and Medina can be found.

Himmat; gh 86 ; literally this means 'striving', but can also refer to the spiritually energetic look directed forcefully by a mystic. Austin describes it as directed use of the creative imagination of the Gnostic. Shah Wali Ullah in speaking of the creation of Eve (Huwa) describes it as arising from the concentrated desire Adam taking on actual physical form.

Hoo, Hu or Ho;, variants on the Arabic word used to denote the ipseity of the Divinity. Allah being the name of the Essence of God, *Hu* though untranslatable (sometimes He is used), has no gender. Described sometimes as implying the Personality of God. *Ho* is used to denote the Jamali nature of God (Beautiful, Loving, and Compassionate) whereas *Hu* or *Hoo* refers to the Jalali nature of God (Majestic and Powerful).

Huma; An auspicious legendary bird – it was said that on whoever the bird's shadow fell would become a king.

Huri/Houri; many ghazals: 'Silver-limbed' beautiful females of paradise.

Idol/idol worship; many ghazals; Hafiz Saheb uses the term in different ways - most frequently in relations to beauties. These are idols in as much as their beauty apparently attracts one away from the worship of One God, but in fact Hafiz sees beyond this – they are a manifestation of God's Beauty and seen in this way are not really idols. Khawaja Muinuddin Hasan Chishti describes idol worship in this way; "Idol worship is this, that the pilgrims on the way may treat pride and fame as the mark of perfection and the pinnacle of glory." The Sufis generally regard self-worship as the real idolatry.

Ihram; gh 68; this is the two unstitched cotton sheets worn by Muslim pilgrims to Mecca whilst performing the circling of the Kaaba.

Iram; gh 55: Qur'an 89.6, but in legend a city built to imitate paradise. The builder was destroyed for his presumption.

Isa/Eesa; gh22: Lord Jesus. Regarded as a prophet by Muslims.

Jam/Jamshid: .a (probably mythical) Persian King associated in mysticism with a goblet in which the whole world can be seen; amongst Sufis thought of as 'the divine mirror'.

Jesus breath; many ghazals: health or life giving breath as Lord Jesus was associated with many healing miracles and raising from the dead.

Jinn; many ghazals. One of the creatures made of "smokeless fire"; in other words of a non-material substance. Another is the Pari – renowned for their great beauty. Jinns may be well disposed or mischievous. They are mentioned often in the holy Qur'an and linked to man in having some degree of will. See Sura an-Nas. They are popular figures in fairy stories such as Aladdin..

Kaaba; gh33: The House of Allah, found in Mecca, Saudi Arabia; the object of pilgrimage for Muslims at least once in their lifetime if possible. A simple cube shaped building around which circumambulations are performed by pilgrims.

Kaf; many ghazals: A mystic mountain and home of the Anka/Anqa.

Kalandar (Qalandar); gh58: A wandering Dervish inclined to ecstatic states and unconventional ways.

Karun; gh36: a man of vast wealth at the time of Moses, he is reported as having been sucked into the sands and it is believed this is in perpetuity.

Kauther (Kawther); gh 55: This refers to a fountain in paradise.

Kerbala/Karbala; gh 13: A battle in which Hz. Hussein the grandson of the holy Prophet was martyred. (10th Muharrem AD 680), Kerbala is in present day Iraq. Hz Hussein had refused allegiance to Yazid and was defeated by a much larger force after being denied even water. The event is commemorated with much sorrow to this day.

Khanqah; gh 54: the lodge or hospice of the Sufis – at times these could be richly decorated grand buildings.

Khilvatis; many ghazals: Reclusive mystics.

Khirqa; gh 136: The cloak or coat passed from the Sufi Sheikh to a disciple carrying with it spiritual blessings.

Khizr; many ghazals: Possibly a temporary guide of the Prophet Moses (see Qur'an 18;65, where he is not named) and of certain other Prophet's and Saints. A helper in difficulty; a friend of God.

Kohl; gh12, 29: black eye-liner used to beautify and enhance the eyes.

Lailat-i-Qadr; see Night of Power.

Lala; gh17: Red poppy-like tulip; appears in spring.

Layla (also Laila, Leyla, etc); gh 87: Literally 'Night' but the name of a woman who was the object of the love of the 'madman' Majnun: so also standing for the Beloved.

Lip; many ghazals: the attraction of divine love; the essence of the soul.

Liver/liver's blood; many ghazals: the liver is the seat of the spiritual faculty governing the body; as such it is associated with grief and difficulty arising from the bodies needs and desires. The drinking of the liver's blood means taking on difficulties that result in spiritual gain, eventually.

Magian(s); many ghazals: The name is associated with the Zoroastrian religion, whose followers were fire-worshippers. The Pir of the Magians is the spiritual master of mystics of that sect.

Majnun; gh 22: literally 'madman' or' lunatic', refers to the lover of Laila/Layla in many tales of the Middle East, and in particular in Sufi literature. Used widely as a model for the crazed lover of God. He is used in Sufi literature to demonstrate various aspects of love. For example he once appeared as a beggar when Laila was distributing water to a queue of beggars. When it came to his turn she refused water. He went away happy. Someone asked why. "Because she singled me out for different treatment from the rest," was his reply.

Mansur (al-Hallaj); gh138: Sufi martyr, executed for declaring 'I am the Truth.'

Marwah (or Marwa); gh91: A small hill adjacent to the Kaaba in Mecca. (see also Safa).

Marut; gh83: one of two fallen angel associated with magic in Babylon. (see also Harut)

Messiah; literally 'the anointed one'. Usually this is referring to Lord Jesus.

Mole; many ghazals: in Hafiz referring to a mole or blemish on the face but regarded as a sign of beauty. Mystically it is the single point of unity encompassing all creation.

Mihrab; gh83, 86, 102 and many others: usually an arch enabling the worshipper to face in the direction of Mecca. Compared frequently to the eyebrow by Hafiz. See also under *Arch.*

Mirror; the mystics mirror enables him or her to see events in the unseen; also events can be seen in the physical world in the mirror of the heart. The mirror of the intellect sees different levels of the inner life.

Moon; many ghazals: may refer to a beauty (human or divine); also associated with the holy Prophet Muhammed.

Murid; Disciple of a spiritual guide.

Murshid; gh102: The seeker's spiritual guide in the Sufi way of mysticism.

Musk; perfume of exceptional quality found in a gland in the naval of a musk-deer. Symbolically something of great rarity- spiritual essence.

Mustapha; gh54: The chosen one, the holy Prophet Muhammed.

Narcissus; variant of daffodil used by Hafiz to symbolise the drunken eye of the beloved. The colour may be associated with sickness – in the sense of being love-sick. The yellow cup of the flower set against the white petals gives the appearance of an eye.

Night of Power; gh 26,113: A night in which divine blessings descend; frequently associated with certain nights towards the end of Ramadan, the fasting month: the night is called Laylat-i-Qadr in Arabic and is described in the holy Quran as a special mystical night of Peace in which many blessings descend on the one fortunate enough to receive this – until dawn. See the Qur'an sura called by the same name.

Nimrod; gh121: A worldly ruler of ill repute who put Prophet Ibrahim (Abraham) into the fire, but Allah made it experienced as coolness for him.

Parvis; several ghazals. In literature an ancient king who became part of a complex love triangle with Shirin and Farhad.

Peri; many ghazals: Beautiful spirit being from the realm of 'creatures made of smokeless fire'; below the rank of angel; inhabitant of the lowest level of heaven.

Pine-cone; many ghazals: the heart was seen as shaped like a pine cone.

Pir; many ghazals: Sometimes used as synonymous with Sufi elder or Murshid, at other times to indicate a Sufi of higher attainment.

Pir of the Magians; originally the title of pre-Islamic spiritual teacher – according to some this became degraded to meaning the keeper of a tavern – in a derogatory sense – but later regained some credibility as in Hafiz poetry.

Qibla (also Kibla); gh 10, 36: the direction of prayer, often marked by a Mihrab or arch, enabling the Muslim to pray in the direction of Mecca.

Ramadan; many ghazals; the month of fasting between dawn and sunset for Muslims. The word itself means 'consuming fire' (Avery).

Rebab; gh 18, 48: bowed string instrument probably predecessor of the modern violin.

Redbud; many ghazals: see 'Arghavan' above.

Rend/Rind; many ghazals. Usually translated as profligacy; shameless dissoluteness; reckless extravagance; great abundance. Referring to those Sufis who tend towards enthusiasm and extravagance in their devotion to the Beloved (God).

Rizwan; gh 19, 36: Gate keeper of the paradise gardens.

Ruknabad; many ghazals: A river in Shiraz.

Rose; many ghazals; May symbolise the divine or human beloved or the spiritual guide according to context.

Ruby; many ghazals: precious stone thought to have gained its purity from the effect of the sun on stone. A symbol of spiritual transformation.

Saba/Sheba; many ghazals, see also under Solomon. Saba is the state ruled by Bilqis, 'Queen of Sheba'.

Saba breeze/wind; many ghazals: Saba is a breeze that blows at dawn from the east. It is a breeze to which lovers confide their secrets and which, according to Abdul-Razzagh Kashani, is "the Clement Waft" Nafahaat-e-Rahmaaniyeh") that blows from the Spiritual East. Saba takes on many roles in Hafez's poems and is a harbinger that carries good news between lover and beloved. Saba Wind blows slowly and brings the scent of the beloved to Hafez so that he will not stay alone. *(Kia , Ali Asghara and Saghe'i-Saeed) see bibliography.*

Safa; gh 91: One of two small hills (the second is called Marwa) adjacent to the site of the Kaaba in Mecca. Running, or walking urgently, between the two, seven times, forms part of the Hajj pilgrimage. It commemorates the frantic search for water by Abraham's wife that culminated in disclosure of the sacred Zamzam spring. Safa also has the meaning of purity. See also Marwa above.

Salam/asalam aleikum; Salam is usually translated as peace however the word has a broader connotation in Arabic implying both peace and security or safety. Salaam aleikum (peace be upon you) is the initial greeting of Muslims meeting each other and is supposed to precede any other conversation. As-salaam is one of Allah's 99 Beautiful names of Allah.

Saki; many ghazals.The Saki is traditionally a young boy who would serve wine at a party, but it can also be the spiritual guide who gives inspiration. Hazrat Abdul Qadir al-Jillani mentions the holy Prophet saying –"I have seen my Lord in the shape of a most beautiful youth." He goes on to say: "As Allah is beyond all shape and form .... it is interpreted as the manifestation of the Lord's beautiful attributes reflected on the mirror of the pure soul..... this is called the child of the heart.....this reflected image is also a connection between the servant and his Lord."(See also our introduction in this volume).

Sama/Sema; gh127: literally – audition. A state the Sufi may enter during listening to special music under particular conditions – the music concert is often called Sama, but in fact Sama as a state does not actually require formal music. Mevlana Rumi is said to have got this state on hearing the beating of the goldsmith's hammering. Sama need not only involve hearing but other senses such as sight and smell and touch.

Samiri; gh123: One of those who escaped Egypt with Prophet Moses. He had the golden calf made whilst Prophet Moses was away receiving the Ten Commandments and was punished severely. It is assumed he used some form of magic to get the idol to make a sound.

Shariat; gh 92: Religious laws derived from the holy Qur'an and Hadiths (accounts of the sayings and actions of the holy Prophet Muhammed).

Sidhra tree; gh88: It is a very large Tree beyond the seventh heaven. It is named the Sidrat al-Muntahā because there terminates at it whatever ascends from the earth and whatever descends [from heaven] including what comes down from God, (and) waḥy (divine inspiration) and other things besides. *(As-Sa'di, Tafsir, 819) courtesy of Wikipedia.*

Solomon (Sulaiman); gh26: Prophet and king, associated with wisdom and linked to the Queen of Sheba. Many Qur'anic and biblical references.

Sikander; Alexander the Great. Sikander's mirror was a mirror in which could be seen all the events going on in the world – sought by Alexander. See also Jamshid.

Silver-limbed; many ghazals: refers usually to a houri/huri – one of the handmaidens of paradise (see many references in holy Qur'an).

Tariqat; gh28: A stage intermediary between the outward following of divine law (Shariat), and the stage of Truth (Haqiqat). In Shariat one pays the customary charity of 2.5%, in Tariqat one pays 97.5% and keeps only the residue. In Haqiqat everything is given and nothing is reserved (see Meditation of Khwaja Muinuddin Hasan Chishti: Sharib Press 1992). Hafiz summarises Tariqat as "Whatever comes my way is best". It is also called the Way. In it there is deep moral and spiritual struggle; the inner or greater Jihad. It is to pass from form (shariat) to essence, whilst haqiqat can perhaps be described as passing from essence to the substance of essence.

Tasbih; gh132: String of beads that are counted when reciting one of the names of God or some other formulae of remembrance of God. A rosary.

Tavern; many ghazals: can be referring to the Khanqah or hospice where Zikr or hearing music for spiritual purposes or spiritual teaching takes place. May also refer to an inner place experienced in meditation. Khwaja Muinuddin Hasan Chishti says: The real tavern is in the heart. But without the guidance of the perfect spiritual guide the absorbed traveller on the way cannot understand it. The tavern means and implies that in the gambling house of love you may lose your wealth, position, garden, land, and whatever is destined in the universe and in both the worlds. (*From the Meditations of Khwaja Muinuddin Hasan Chishti – Sharib Press 1992, Southampton*)

Temple; many ghazals; "The implication of 'the temple and the place of idol worship' is wide enough to cover even the slightest thought of both the worlds occupying your heart." (*from the Meditations of Khwaja Muinuddin Hasan Chishti – Sharib Press 1992, Southampton*)

Tuba tree; gh19, 22: A tree in Paradise, whose width is a hundred years, and the clothes of the people of Paradise are taken from its bark (Hadith). A place of good return after this life. [www.qtafsir.com]

Turk; many ghazals: varied usage – can refer to the *beloved;* also to a powerful force.

Venus; gh 9: acc to W-C. - Venus (Zuhra) is female singer in the fourth heaven in which the Messiah, Jesus, lives. A propitious planet.

Way, the; many ghazals: Can mean the straightway described in the holy Qur'an, also of course path or road. The Sufi Way – the path on which the Sufi travels to the Beloved (God).The progression through mystical stages of awakening. In English, of course, there is a double meaning since we talk of the 'way' we do something as distinct from *what* we do. This expresses an aspect of what the Way means amongst Sufis – in some respects it is not what is done but the *way* in which it is done that counts.

Wheat; gh24: used in the Qur'an (rather than apple as in bible) as the means of Adam's seduction and fall.

Wine: The real wine in a clear heart is the sign and symbol of moving about in Allah, and refers to the virtues and qualities and to the way of life to be moulded according to the attributes of Allah. The pure and purifying wine is this; that the divine grace may descend upon the heart of the faithful witness of the truth. (*from the Meditations of Khwaja Muinuddin Hasan Chishti – Sharib Press 1992, Southampton*)

Wudhu; gh 27,118: the ritual ablution preceding the Muslim ritual prayer.

Yemen prayer; 100: A prayer taught by the holy Prophet to his son-in- law Hz Ali, when he sent him to Yemen as envoy.

Yemen, (breath coming from); gh 66: probably a reference to a comment of the holy Prophet who speaks of a breath of divine mercy coming from Yemen, and possibly meaning from Uwais Qarni a man whose love of the Prophet, who he did not get to meet physically, caused him to remove his own teeth in sympathy for the hurt done to a tooth of the holy prophet in battle.

Yusuf; many ghazals: Prophet Joseph (see Qur'an - Sura Yusuf, and Biblical accounts).Key features to his story include his ability to interpret dreams, his great physical beauty, his being put down a well by his brothers, his rescue and being sold into slavery, the attempted seduction by Zuleika, the love his father Prophet Yaqub (Jacob) had for him, that caused prophet Yaqub to go blind, the sending of a shirt of Prophet Yusuf that cured the older man of blindness.

Zoroaster/Zarathustra; gh121: Founder of the ancient Zoroastrian religion of Persia in which fire worship is the main feature.

Zuleika (Zuleikha); See holy Qur'an (Sura Yusuf). The wife of the purchaser of Prophet Joseph (Yusuf) when he was enslaved first in Egypt. She fell in love with Yusuf and tried to seduce him – he refused, and was sent to prison falsely accused of assault. Many stories are told in Persian literature of her continued devotion to the Prophet – she therefore is used to represent 'the faithful lover'.

Bibliography

Primary English Sources;

Avery, P.; The Collected Lyrics of Hafiz of Shiraz; Archetype; 2007; ISBN 1-901383-09-1.
Wilberforce-Clarke, H; The Divan. Volumes 1 and 2, The Octagon Press Ltd, London. 1974. SBN 90086018 9.
Sharib, Z H.;The Rubaiyat of Hafiz; Sharib Press; Southampton, 1993; ISBN 0-9508926-5-3.
Smith, P,; Divan of Hafiz; New Humanity Books; 1983; ISBN 0-949-191-00-0.

Secondary English Sources

Anon; Selection of Rubaiyat and Odes; Watkins. Nd.
Arberry, A.J.; Shiraz, Persian City of Saints and Poets; Norman University of Oaklahoma Press; 1960; no ISBN.
Alston; In Search of Hafiz; Shanti Sadan: 1996: 0 854244 045 4
Avery P., and J. Heath-Stubbs, Hafiz of Shiraz, London, 1952.
Bell, G.; Teachings of Hafiz; Octagon Press, London; 1979; ISBN 90086063 4
Gray, E. T. (1995). The Green Sea of Heaven. Ashland: White Cloud Press.
Idem, Fifty Poems of Hafiz, Text and Translations, Cambridge, 1947.
Jamshidipur, Y.; Selected Poems of Hafiz; Tehran; 1963.
Ladinski, D.; The Gift,;Arkana 1999; ISBN 0 14 01.9581 5
*Loloi, P.;*Hafiz, Master of Persian Poetry; I.B.Taurus; New York; 2004.
MacCarthy, Ghazels from the Divan of Hafiz done into English, London, 1893.
Nicholson, R.A; Translations of Eastern Poetry and Prose; Curzon Press Ltd., London. 1987. ISBN 0 70070196 6.
*Saberi, R,;*The Divan of Hafiz; A Bilingual text, Persian-English.. UPA. Lanham/ New York/ Oxford. 2002. ISBN 0-7618-2246-1.
Sahlepour, S. Divan of Hafiz; Booteh Press, Tehran; 1998. ISBN 964-90021-5-4.
Salami, I,; The Divan of Hafiz; Tehran, 2013.ISBN 978-964-8741-55-1.

Smith, P.; Tongue of the Hidden; New Humanity Books;. 1974: 0 949191 05 1
Smith, P; Introduction to Divan of Hafiz; New Humanity Books: 1986: 0 949 191 00 0
Smith, P.; Loves Perfect Gift; New Humanity Books. 1988: 0 949191 04 3

On-line English sources

Zahuri Sufi Web Site – www.zahuri.org – see Persian Pages
http://www.hafizonlove.com/bio/
http://www.iranonline.com/literature/hafez/one.html
http://www.majzooban.org/en/articles/3178-shams-al-din-hafez-shirazi-great-poet-of-persia.html
http://en.wikipedia.org/wiki/Hafez
http://www.thesongsofhafiz.com/life.htm Primary Farsi Sources;
http://www.iranicaonline.org/articles/hafez-x
http://www.academicjournals.org/article/article1379490294_Bahrami.pdf
https://coursewikis.fas.harvard.edu/aiu18/Hafez
http://islam.uga.edu/sufipoetry.html

Farsi Resources

Khoramshahi ,B.:Hafez Name;Tehran 2011.ISBN 978-964-445-175-1
Shojaeeadib,Sh,;The Divan of Hafiz; Khatere majmoo;2003,ISBN 964-7020-10-4
Divan-e Khajeh Shamseddin Mohammad Hafiz-e Shirazi, *by Mohammad Ghazvini and Dr. Ghasem Ghani (in Persian)*
Divan-e Hafiz-e Shirazi, *by Dr. Seyyed Mohammad Reza Jalaly Nayeenii (in Persian)*
Divan-e Khajeh Shamseddin Mohammad Hafiz-e Shirazi, *compiled by Mohammad Jaafar Mahjoobi (in Persian)*
Divan-e Khajeh Shamseddin Mohammad Hafiz-e Shirazi (revised and elucidated); Dr.Parviz Natel Khanlari.

On-line Farsi Resources

http://ganjoor.net/hafez/
http://hafezdivan.blogpars.com/
http://www.1doost.com/hafez/omen/

Some books related to Sufism

Akhtar/Taher; Sufi Saints; Anmol Publications; 1998: 81 7488 939 6*Atta Illah/Danner;* Sufi Aphorisms (Kitab al-Hikam); E.J.Brill. Leiden; 1973: 90 04 07168 7

Atta Illah/Danner; Book of Wisdom: SPK (La).

Arabi/Bursevi Kernel of Kernels Beshara. nd.

 *Arabi/Austin;*The Sufis of Andalusia ; Beshara ;1971; 0 904 975 13 4

Arabi/Austin; The Bezels of Wisdom; Paulist Press; 1980   0 8091 2331 2 (pr) 0 8091 0313 3 (cl)

*Arabi/Weir ; W*hosoever Knoweth Himself; Beshara;1976; 0 904975 06 1

Arberry. ;Kalabadhi/y ;The Doctrine of the Sufis Muhammad Ashraf 1966

Arabi/Burkhardt ; Hisbul-l-Wiqayah   Ibn Arabi Society ; Beshara; 1977 ; 0 904975 09 6
*Arberry, A.*Classical Persian Literature; Curzon   1994   0 7007 0276 8

Attar/Darbandi; Conference of the Birds; Penguin: 1988: 0-14-044434-3

Attar/Arberry: Muslim Saints and Mystics; Arkana: 1990: 0 14 019264 6

Babajan/Shepherd ; A Sufi Matriarch; Anthropographia Publications, Camb: 1985: 0 9508680 1 9

*Baldick,;*Mystical islam: I. B. Tauris;1989   1 85043 137 X : 1 85043 140 X

Bistami/Sells ; Early Islamic Mysticism ; Paulist Press ; 1996   0-8091-0477-6 (cloth)

Brown, E.G.: The Dervishes: Frank Cass & Co. 1968

Chittick ,W.; Sufi Path of Knowledge; S. Univ. N.York: 1989: 0 88706 885 5 (p) 0 88706 884 7

Danner/Kingsley; Quest for Red Sulphur; Islamic Text Soc. 1993;   0 946621 45 4)p) 0 946621 4 4 6 cl

Ernst, C.: Words of Ecstasy in Sufism ; SUNY; 1985; 0 87395-917-5

Ernst, C; Eternal Garden; SUNY Press 1992; 0-7914-0883-30-7 914-0884-1(pbk)

*Ernst, C.;*Shambala Guide to Sufism;Shambala: 1997: 1 57062 180 2

Ernst, C. Ruzbihan Baqli - Rhetoric of Sainthood in Persian Sufism; Curzon Press;1996; 0 7007 0342 X

Fadiman/Frager; Essential Sufism; Harper; San Fransisco ; 1997; 0 06 251474 1 (cl) 0 06 251475 x (pb)

Harris ; Journey to the Lord of Power; Inner Traditions Int.; 1980; 089281 024 6

Hujwiri/Nicholson; Kashf al-Mahjub ; Luzac & Co.;1976 ; 0 7189 0203 3

Husaini; Pantheistic Monotheism of Ibn Arabi; Ashraf ..

Lawrence; Notes from a Distant Flute Coombe Springs Press. 1978. 0 9508926 9 6.

Lewishon; The Heritage of Sufism Vol 2; One World: 1992: 1-85168-189-2

Lewis; Rumi - Past and Present, East and West One World (Oxford); 2000 ISBN. 1 85168 214 7.

Lings, M.; What is Sufism; 1975.

Nicholson R.A.; Personality in Sufism; Adam Publishers: 1998: 81 7435 142 6

*Nicholson R.A.;*Studies in Islamic Mysticism; Cambridge Uni. Press 1989 . ISBN 0 521 29546 7

Nizami; Life & Times of Nasiruddin Chirag; Idarah-i-Adabyat-i-Delli: 1991:

Rastogi; Islamic Mysticism Sufism; East West: 1982: 0 856 92 096 7

Rumi/Nicholson; The Masnavi (6 bks in 3 vols);Gibb Memorial Trust;1990: 0 906094 10 0 (3rd vol).

Schimmel A.; Deciphering the Signs of God; SUNY: 1994: 0 7914 1982 7

*Schimmel A.;*As Through a Veil:Mystical Poetry in Islam; New York 1982.

Sells,; Early Islamic Mysticism; Paulist Press: 1996.

Sharib Z.H.;Reflections of the Mystics of Islam; Sharib Press; 1995; 0 9508926 9 6

*Sharib Z.H.;*Ghous-ul-Azam Piran-e-Pir ;Asma; 1961

Sharib Z.H.; The Culture of the Sufis; Sharib Press; Southampton; 1999. 0 9531517 1 9

Sharib: The Sufi Saints of the Indian Subcontinent; Munshiram Manoharlal; Delhi. 2006. ISBN: 81-215-1052-X.

Sharib, Z.H.; Khwaja Gharib Nawaz;Muhammad Ashraf: 1990: none

*SharibZ.H.;*Ghous-ul-Azam Piran-e-Pir; Asma: 1961:

Sharib Z.H. Reflections of the Mystics of Islam   Sharib Press; 1995; 0 9508926 9 6.

as-Sulami/Cornell; Early Sufi Women; Fons Vitae: 1999: 1-887752 06 4

Sushud/Holland; The Masters of Wisdom of C. Asia; Coombe Springs Press; 1983: 0 900306 93 9

Syed Ali Reza Najul Bhalaga (Peak of Eloquence)   Tahrika ;Tarsil Qur'an, Inc ;1985:   0 940368 43 9   0 940368 42 0

Trimingham; The Sufi Orders in Islam; OU Press 1971

Troll (ed) Muslim Shrines in India; Oxford Uni. Press : 1989 :

Waliullah/Baljon; Mystical Interpretation of Prophetic Tales; Brill - Leiden: 1973: 90 04 03833 7

Waliullah/Jalbani; The Lamahat and Sata'at; Octagon Press: 1980: 9008 6081 2
*Waliullah/Jalbani;*The Sacred Knowledge; Octagon Press: 1982: 90086093 6

Publications by **Sharib Press** of books by Dr Zahurul Hasan Sharib available at www.zahuri.org
The Psalm of Life/The Psalm of Love/ The Psalm of Light/ The Meditations of Khwaja Moinuddin Hasan Chishti/Abu Said Abi'l Khair and his Rubaiyat/ Hafiz and his Rubaiyat/Sarmad and his Rubaiyat/The Culture of the Sufis/Reflection of the Mystics of Islam/Qur'anic Prayers/Qur'anic Precepts/Qur'anic Parables.

Appendix: Volume 4

W-C 454
Additional lines in Khanlari (as footnote) and in W-C.
The ray of beauty became a veil to the eye of comprehension,
Come and make the pavilion of the sun full of illumination.

The sugar lump of union with you is more than I am greedy for,
To be taken to the ruby lip as sweet as sugar is what I look for.

Kiss the lip of the cup then pass it on to the inebriated,
With this subtlety make the companions minds scented.

Beloved, on account of your fine qualities and sweet inclinations,
Lift up your head like the candle in the feast of the companions.

W-C 465
Holy is the bird of my heart, the ninth heaven its residency,
It's fed up with the world and with the body's cage is angry.

How the bird flies from the top of this pile of dust,
At the entrance to that door the falcon makes its nest.

When the bird of the heart flees, its home is the lofty Sidrah tree,
The top of the ninth heaven our falcon's resting place must be.

The shadow of fortune falls on the head of all the world,
If it spreads its feathers and wings over the world.

It lives only above the sphere not in this world or the other,
The body's origin is the mine, the soul comes from nowhere.

The highest sphere is the place of our bird's splendid showing,
From the rose-bed of the beloved water and food it is getting.

Crazed Hafiz! Since you speak so much about God's unity,
On the page of both Man and Jinn draw with your pen of unity.

W-C 467
If from the rock of Badakhshan there emerges a ruby,
From the gorge like sugar out comes the water of the Rukni,

From every household's door in Shiraz city,
Comes out a heart-ravishing coquettish beauty.

From the house of religious leaders of every description,
There comes out the rose-coloured wine without adulteration.
From the pulpit when in hypocritical ecstasy they shout,
From the expounder's turban the (scent of) cannabis comes out.

In the gardens, with the singer's voice, mornings and evenings,
Comes out the bulbul's lament and the striking of the harp's strings.

In such a city, separated from the beloved and grieving,
From his house Hafiz comes out, with a heart that is hurting.
(W-C 476) *(W-C only)*
When the beloved's hair's trap scattered hearts into the dust that way,
What came the way of our sorry, sad, heart - out of love say.

Last night, at my moaning, the meadow's bird cried copiously,
Breeze, if you know what eventually happened then, tell me.

Though we are bad do not think of us that way,
Speak about the beggar's sin in a royal way.

(W-C 477) *(W-C only)*
In the heart's field one who is not made green by fidelity,
At their own harvest time they will reap a yellow face only.

 Be like the rings in the tambourine and in that circle stay,
Whatever beating you get, from that circle don't go away.

W-C 478a
Sweet singer your sweet refrain sing again renew, anew,
Efforts to find the heart-expanding wine renew, anew.

With a beauty dressed like a doll sit in a private place,
Your desire to take from her a kiss renew, anew.

My silver-legged Saki is not here, bring me fresh wine,
For the wine-jug's contents I would quickly renew, anew.

When do you enjoy life's fruit then, if you don't drink wine?
To that one's memory drink wine and wine drinking renew, anew.

The heart-ravishing one, for me, will
Decoration, adornment, colour and perfume renew, anew.

O morning breeze, when you pass over the street of that Peri,
To her be telling the story of Hafiz, it renew, anew.

W-C 481
The evil heart do not keep. For you also reach to the day of union,
Because you have tasted the poison of the night of separation.

May the evil eye be far from you, for in the decoration of heart-ravishing,
On the beauty of Yusuf of Canaan a line you are drawing.

Again, my foot is not touching the ground, happily,
Since you have looked towards me benignly.

You fancifully ask after lovers who have nothing,
As if in them the scent of fidelity you are getting.

W-C 482
O you, whose splendid face lights the lamp of the eye,
The world never saw the like of your intoxicated eye.

One dear as you, filled with graciousness from head to toe,
The world has not seen nor has the Lord made it to be so.

This eye and that eyebrow, after the lover's blood wishing to go,
Sometimes this would set a trap, or that would shoot the arrow.

How long, like a half-dead fowl should the heart's dove be?
That in blood and dust by the arrow of separation it was made be.

From my heart's fire smoke rises up constantly,
How long like aloes-wood on the fire shall I be?

If you don't take my hand then to the Khwaja I will go, saying,
That from the hapless lovers their heart and eyes you were taking.

The above lines are in Khanlari volume two. The ones below are in W-C.

Every zahid who saw your ruby, wine-selling,
Took up the wine cup and the prayer carpet was abandoning.

If for your cheek the eyebrow has no inclination,
How come it is always bowed like my body's position.

If you place your lip on mine, immortal life I gain,
The instant to your lip my sweet life may attain.

At your foot the thorn of separation has fallen in confusion,
And no rose is ever plucked from the rose-bed of union.

This is our stock-in-trade, if to your taste it is,
Write in book the pearls of Hafiz.

(W-C 484) *Two additional lines in W-C only.*
The cup of delight was taken up by the angel of mercy,
Who threw from its dregs rosewater over Houri and Peri.

The new crescent moon, in hope of serving his mount as a horseshoe,
From the ninth heaven to ground beneath (the king) a hundred kisses blew.

(W-C 486) *Additional lines only in W-C.*
Sweet yet eloquent in enunciation; elegantly tall and full of beauty,
A gracious and heart-catching face; an arrow-eye, drawn and ready.

Many thanks I would say, if my service to the elder,
Into my hand the fruit that's ripe and ready it deliver.

You heard every evil spoken about us by the enemy,
O Lord! Cut short may the tongue of the adversary be.

(W-C 487) *(W-C only)*
Give a vessel of wine so I can come out, maybe,
From this stream whose shores I cannot see.

From union with a beauty who gained anything,
When love of their own self was their thing.

Drink wine, for in this house there is no stranger,
O peerless man, except you, there is no other.

(W-C 489) Additional lines in W-C only.
Nothing is more pleasant than the lover's patience,
Patience seek from God; from Him seek patience.

The patched robe is a cord on the Way,
Sufi! Cast aside this practice and this way.

Once from the face of the beloved I had good times,
In union I expressed my wonder a hundred times.

I do not turn my face from the way of the beloved's service,
Never raised up from the dust of that court my head is.

(W-C 490)
Heartbroken Hafiz would not have been this way,
If he had listened to what the wine-seller had to say.

(W-C 491)
It is Eid and the season of the rose! O Saki bring wine,
Whoever in the rose season saw a cup without wine?

My heart is contracted by all this hypocritical austerity,
So that it may be expanded, give some wine O Saki.

The Sufi who yesterday counselled the lovers to pray,
I saw him drunk and casting piety to the wind today.

An extra day or two of the rose season take as a bonus,
If you are a lover from the face of the Saki seek to be joyous.

The rose has gone why do you sit carelessly O friends of mine,
With no harp's sound, no beloved and no cup of wine?

You know in the cup's morning assembly how good it is to see,
Fallen into the wine cup the reflection of the cheek of the Saki.

When the musician strikes a chord, if possible his song will be one,
About the elegance of Hafiz's verse at the banquet of a royal son.

(W-C 492)
Since God has made it my fate to be a tavern sitter,
O puritan, where is there sin for me in this matter.

Before time began, one to whom the cup of wine was given,
On Judgement Day how should they hold this against him then.

Say, to the hypocritical, two-faced, patched-robe wearing Sufi,
Whose practice to be long handed and short sleeved could it be?

For hypocrisy's sake you continue to wear patched robe anyway,
So that with your blue clothes you can lead God's slaves astray.

I am the slave of the Rend's headless and footless spirit,
Less than a straw the two worlds are for those who have it.

Since in the tavern I could fulfil what I intend,
In college and cloister my face is blackened.

Hafiz, go and don't beg at every beggars door,
Or, unless God Wills it, you won't get what you seek for.

W-C 494
(There is one additional line in W-C and Qani);
Though river Zinda (of Isfahan) is life's water,
Yet our Shiraz compared to Isfahan, is better.

W-C 501 *(W-C only)*
What difference does my ignorance and your knowledge make to the sky,
What does ugliness or beauty matter, when, to see it, there is no eye.

Your pen! May its sweet tongue always powerful be,
There is no love from you, else salaam you'd have written me.

If you were not coloured with love by the Divine Artificer,
He would not have mixed Adams clay with love's water.

(W-C 504) *additional lines in W-C*
O you who, in union with the heart's ease, choose privacy,
In the moment when you have great desire, profit see.

Though in the case of fidelity you are not steady,
You are stable with regard to violence, thanks be.

Kind became the sky since it abandoned violent activity,
O soul, you are one who, in this respect, is moved strongly.

W-C 506 (W-C only)
No violence comes from the sky whilst you have kingly quality,
Oppression left the world since you became its canopy.

In the household of Adam as long as there is sovereignty,
No one knows better than you the way it should be.

O shelter for created beings! O gift giver!
On one poor as I am, be the mercy giver.

W-C 512
*There is some difficulty in establishing the verses here. Avery and Saberi do include
this. W-C has different verses from those we could locate in Farsi. As this presentation
of Hafiz makes no claim to scholarship of any kind we include just a sample of the
verses in this appendix.*

O heart, void of love and intoxication never ever be,
Then go, for from non-being and being, you'll be free.

Every idol you see, in service of that one be,
Better than self worship any other Qibla must be.

The sign of disbelieving is being raw, in Tariqat s creed,
Yes, the way to fortune is found in expertise and speed.

As long as you see virtue and intellect you are deprived of gnosis,
One point I must tell you; in not seeing yourself freedom there is.

W-C 515
A glance by a tranquil heart at a moon-faced beauty,
Is better than a king's crown and a life of anxiety.

By God I feel jealous of my own eye that sees your face,
For there is something to pity in looking at such a tender face.

My heart gone, and I know not what happened to that dear one,
Our life has passed and no news came from any direction.

My breath expired but I didn't see that one fully,
No other desire than this lingers on in me.

O breeze do not ruffle so wildly my beloved's hair,
Hafiz would give a thousand lives for just one hair.

W-C 521
The value of the dust of that one's foot apparent would be,
If precious life were to last for more than eternity.

If the image of you no barrier to my eye's water had been,
In every corner a thousand fountains there would have been.

O God, that a sign of the beloved's street someone had given me,
So that from dependence on rose and garden I would have been free.

(This verse is not translated by Avery but is a footnote in Khanlari.)
Even in sleep I don't see that one, what chance then of union,
Being without this, I would to God that the other there had been.

W-C 522
(alternate to verse one)
If you are sitting at the edge of a stream full of self-illusion,
Then any calamity you see arises from your own self delusion.

Additional verses in W-C
After this, me and beggary are together, for in love's way,
There is no remedy but wretchedness for followers of this way.

A morning breeze arose in the garden, desiring you,
For like the wild white rose and the scented red are you.

W-C 524 *additional verses in W-C.*
Speak with wine of sorrow on the calamitous death day,
At such a time one cannot trust in any other anyway.

With a happy heart sit in a corner, and see,
No one keeps in mind this strange calamity.

In the hand of the mean observer my beloved I see,
So it is the sky takes revenge on the service of one like me.

I have heard placed by you on dogs a collar there is,
So why not then a rope on the neck of Hafiz?

W-C 527
(An additional line in a footnote of Khanlari).
You have to give your entire fortune of gold and silver,
To satisfy your greed for those whose limbs are silver.

These lines are in W-C only
Both heart and faith have gone; but but what is there to say,
For regarding them in my heart you keep burning away.

You who in the colourful rags of the Sufi, God's presence seek
Really! From those who know nothing fulfilment you seek?

(W-C 534) *(additional verses in W-C)*
Union with chaste women age is preventing,
Save the kissing of the cheek and hugging.

It is not our lot – to be with friends uniting,
Hafiz, the ghazals of Iraq be singing.

(W-C 535) *(additional verses in W-C)*
Tie your heart to Laila's hair and work with Majnun's reason,
Because, for lovers, injury speaks words of reason.

The magic of the tempting glance is pain and a remedy giver,
In the musk scented hair is the heart's enslaver and its easer.

(W-C 544) *(additional verses in W-C)*
Well mannered sovereign rider, how sweet a doll you are,
That before the eye you appear, though out of sight you are.

The path of love is such a very dangerous one, really,
God give us refuge! If you don't find the way to safety.

W-C 545
In sorrow for you, by us, eternal union by us can be got,
In love for you I have spent my life, but I care not.

What ease they each have, the dogs of your street,
Oh that I only I could be someplace near that street.

O beloved! From my tear came revelation of my mystery,
O you who know this, my state – on my tear have pity!

O all you pure players. Lovely ones don't have fidelity,
From one who possesses beauty don't expect fidelity.

Though our lip is thirsty, we have passed the water of life by,
O Saki with a drop of the clear water our thirst satisfy.

From desire for you I gave up religion and the world too,
Love of status and wealth I gave up in my desire for you.

If in the dust of your doorstep Hafiz's death should be,
Truly he will gain the life that lasts for all eternity.

W-C 546
In front of you from shame the red rose is dripping sweat,
In front of your red lip the cup of wine is full of sweat.

Is it dew on the tulip? On the rose, rose-water is it?
Is it water on fire? On your face perspiration is it?

You with the arch shaped eyebrow went from my view,
My heart followed after but kept losing track of you.

Tonight I will not let go of your hair,
O caller to prayer go, and call to prayer.

As with Majnun's tribe many would go off their head,
If Layla were to return to life (from the tribe of the dead).

On the lip of the musician the reed flute was placed,
Under the fingernail it is right the harp string is placed.

For a while put the harp in the hand of the musician,
And say, "Strum on its string and let it make exultation".

Light up the incense-burner and incense be burning,
From the cold of a winter day do not be in suffering.

Bring out the wine cup and like Hafiz don't eat suffering,
Why to agonise about when Jamshid or Kaus were living.

One who, to get a drop (of wine), his life will give,
Accept all that he has and a cup to that one give.

From now on, if for you the sphere turns unkindly
In the presence of the ruler of Rai declare it boldly.

The king who opens such new horizons on generosity,
That even the famed record of Hatim Tai closed must be.

W-C 547
Bring wine and free me from this hangover of mine,
For one can drive away the hangover with more wine.

In love's gathering the light of the lamp does not shine,
Except in the face of the beloved and wine from the vine.

Do not take pride in the sorcery of your seductive look,
For I have tried it, and from haughtiness no profit I took.

Precept giver, you say a lot about avoiding love play,
But no one can lay down precepts about this, I say.

Alive with love is the soul of a man who has a heart,
If you have no love, go, you're excused for your part.

With a single act of deception I let all probity go.
All that chastity, austerity and that probity – Oh!

The fortune of union came, the pain of separation did not remain,
The country of the heart turned its face toward prosperity again.

Hafiz, one cannot tell to all and sundry the heart's mystery,
Tell only one who has suffered from separation's misery.

W-C 548
O breeze the scent of the beloved you carry,
From that one a musky perfume you have to carry.

Hey, don't you go reaching out such a lot,
With that one's hair what business have you got.

Sweet basil! You and that one's down, are where?
That one is fresh; but you have a hangover.

Narcissus! You and that one's intoxicated eye, are where?
That one is light headed; you have a heavy hangover!

Cypress! With that one's great height what's to compare?
A far as the garden goes; what standing do you have there?

Wisdom! With that one's love there is no comparison,
What power do you have that you can put your hand on.

Hafiz! One day union you will have,
If the power of patience you can have.

W-C 549
Appearing are the ways of infidelity,
No one now carries the sign of fidelity.

To the miser they go now from poverty -
The skilled ones – with the beggar's plea.

These days the ones who have fine qualities,
From grief even momentarily have no ease.

But it is the fool who is wealthy presently,
Since his goods at this time have currency.

If from the poet flows the finest poetry,
That provide for the heart a light to see –

From greed they give him not as much as a pea,
Even if like the great poet Sanai that one may be.

Yesterday wisdom whispered in my ear, continually,
"Go be patient when no resources there appear to be."

Make contentment your stock in trade and your ration
Since without any means you are in pain and affliction.

Hafiz come, in your soul my counsel understand,
If from your foot you fall on your head you land.

W-C 550
O puritan go with the hope you carry,
For like you hopefulness I also carry.

Save the cup what does the tulip have in the hand,
Saki! Come and bring whatever you have at hand.

Draw me into the thread of those who are crazy,
For intoxication is far nicer than sense to me.

O Sufi, shun me, near me do not be coming,
For I declare I have repented of abstaining.

Come, to that one's curls, your heart be attaching,
If to escape to freedom is what you are seeking.

For God's sake in the rose season destroy penitence,
For the rose season has not got any permanence.

O my Friends! The freshness of spring has passed on,
As the spring breeze from the meadow border has gone.

Hafiz, come and drink wine the colour of ruby,
Your life passed in heedlessness, why should it be?

(W-C 551) *(W-C has one additional line.)*

When you recall that one's the ruby lip, and you hear
That sweet tale, turned to sugar is whatever in your mouth you have.

W-C 553
My soul is sacrifice for you; who are both soul and beloved to me,
My head is sacrifice for you; else in a spin it is, with the rest of me.

To rise from the top of your street, I cannot do easily,
They do not accept with ease work of such difficulty.

The raw ones, the power of a wing scorched moth are not possessing,
The delicate ones have no access to the way of soul surrendering.

From immaturity comes sitting at ease, without you,
From amazement comes sitting coquettishly with you.

The mystery of the heart your guardians revealed,
How can such a great mystery remain unconcealed?

So that your tall figure, like a plant, remain nice and healthy,
It is necessary that planted in my (wet) eye you should be.

One day I saw my heart in the curl of your hair,
I said, "How is it, how is the prisoner doing there?"

My heart replied, "Yes, what can you do except envy me,
It's not every poor beggar has a great king's rank, like me"

Hafiz, truly you have not yet reached the limit of our society,

It's enough that at the top of our street you keep dogs company.

W-C 554
As today, in the world of beauty, you are ruling,
Perhaps your lip may stimulate the lovers longing.

How long will you treat with disdain those who have lost their heart to you?
How long only violence and contempt will those wretches get from you?

How long will your eye the cause of powerlessness be,
How long twisting and turning in your hair will they be.

If a little of the pain and violence that you visited on me,
You knew, I know that you would show mercy to me.
The goods for being a lover require capital aplenty;
Hearts that burn like fire; eyes that an ocean seem to be.

Left in separation I was! O dawn breeze carry,
From the garden of union the scent of union to me.

If, on resurrection day, hope of union with you, life is giving,
Yet from shame my head from the dust I will not be bringing.

If a drop of the wine of union with you I should be drinking,
I will not practise being a sensible one, so long as I am living.

A powerful ruler you are, only powerless slaves are we;
Whether by force you bring me or with contempt kill me.

In the end, for the bitter state of Hafiz have some pity,
How long hopelessness? How long will this distress be?

W-C 555
Saki, if you have the desire for wine,
Then I say bring nothing to us but wine.

The Sufi cloak and the prayer carpet,
Sell in the tavern. A drop of wine to get.

If your heart is alive, from you, the intoxicated one,
In the rose bed of your soul, hear "O Living One!"

If you have sorrow as a possession – come to the remedy,
Take both worlds to be nothing - if you possess iniquity.

In the Way of love the heart's mysteries are the following,
The harp strings resonant sound and the reed flute's crying.

In the Way of love one who is poor and pure,
Is better than a thousand Hatim Tai's for sure.

That angel faced idol, like royalty is coming,
Following behind, the city folk are coming.

At her beautiful face men are looking
And at her cheek from shyness sweating.

Separations grief; how long will Hafiz have to complain about,
The end of the breaking heart, when will it come about.

W-C 556
No place more pleasant than the street of the tavern can there be,
Even if for my grey head a more sumptuous abode there could be.

Why should I keep hidden from you this desire of mine,
For a beautiful companion; a pleasure palace; a flagon of wine.

My place is where Magians pray and the meadows of my own country,
My pleasure is the face of idols, which is a fortunate choice by me.

Be respectful regarding the praying place not just anybody can say,
Its affairs are only known to an ardent officer or a great Rai.

O idol, in our heart where is there other than you?
For I have a care for nothing except for you.

Take pity on the wounded hurting heart of Hafiz,
For after today its certain a terrible tomorrow there is.

W-C 561 (additional lines not in all versions)

On account of your stature the cypress is left standing,
Move well, for in travel, the cypress you're exceeding.

O do not drive poor grief stricken Hafiz away from you,
He gave heart, religion and youth for love of the face of you.

W-C 562 *(verses not in Avery or Saberi)*
Its throne from retirement to the garden the rose was bringing,
In the manner of the rosebud the carpet of austerity be folding.

Like that one's eye don't let the drinker intoxicated be,
O Saki give wine in memory of that one's lip of ruby.

The soul does not seek separation from that body,
If the blood of the cup runs through its veins and body.

When that "Hu, Hu," comes from the bird of the early morning,
Do not let the wine cup of Hai, Hai, from your grasp be slipping.

Like Majnun when for the sight of his beloved Laila searching,
O heart everyone in the tribe of Hayy you must move be moving

With the Sultan of the rose drink wine and be happy,
Take profit in being free from December in January.

W-C 568 *(alternate translation for 8th verse)*
The barrel busting guardian does not know the value to the Sufi,
Of a household article – in the pomegranate form, there is a ruby.

(W-C 570) *(W-C only)*
You should enter the hut of grieving lovers, for a moment,
And at night the consoler of my sorrowful heart you should be.
(W-C 571) *(W-C only)*
My heart turned to blood in the hand of that one when in to my memory,
Came that drunken eye. Injury on injury, what has love to do with me?

If you are to be disposed to turn to me, it's now or never,
On one side the lover; the knowing seeker on the other.

O camel drivers who have departed from my residence,
Tell the men of Najd my state if you meet by coincidence
.

In loving, my blood was seen as fair game by the heart-ravisher,
O you gathering of Lords what's decided by love, the decision maker.

Desiring the men of Najd, this eye sleep did not attain,
This enraptured heart melted away in severe pain.

For the sake of God! In that desert my beloved was where?
Wisdom up and run away when it saw the deer that was there.

(W-C 572) *(W-C only)*
Subsequently, to you we have to advance our soul,
For you fought fiercely with lovers and their heart stole.

(W-C 573) *(W-C only)*

A mirror to your singleness the light of God does offer,
Enter by our door, if its everlasting love you are after.

Give wine, for if the name of our sin hell were to call out,
With water, the miracle of Muhammed1 puts the fire out.

Every moment you practise magic, but this is not lawful I say,
The messenger of our Lord has said, "Tricks we never play".

If you pass by the garden in all your grace and glory,
The lily, the cypress and the rose following you will be.

Why do you draw the sword of malice with vicious intent to me,
You do not have in mind "Extended lofty columns of fire" maybe.

In time clean from the tablet of the heart the image of selfhood,
If to take the path of wisdom with heart and soul you would.

The bird of your heart is trapped in the net of desires, Hafiz,
Don't boast of singleness when with you shame there is.

www.ingramcontent.com/pod-product-compliance
Lightning Source LLC
Chambersburg PA
CBHW031952080426
42735CB00007B/359